MATHEMATICS ASSESSMENT

MATHEMATICS ASSESSMENT

What Works in the Classroom

Gerald Kulm

Jossey-Bass Publishers
San Francisco

Substantial discounts on bulk quantities of Jossey-Bass books
are available to corporations, professional associations, and other
organizations. For details and discount information, contact the
special sales department at Jossey-Bass Inc., Publishers.
(415) 433-1740; Fax (415) 433-0499.

For international orders, please contact your local Paramount Publishing
International office.

Manufactured in the United States of America. Nearly all Jossey-Bass
books and jackets are printed on recycled paper that contains at least
50 percent recycled waste, including 10 percent postconsumer waste.
Many of our materials are also printed with vegetable-based inks;
during the printing process these inks emit fewer volatile organic
compounds (VOCs) than petroleum-based inks. VOCs contribute to
the formation of smog.

Library of Congress Cataloging-in-Publication Data

Kulm, Gerald.
   Mathematics assessment : what works in the classroom / Gerald
Kulm.
      p. cm. — (The Jossey-Bass education series)
  Includes bibliographical references and index.
    ISBN 0-7879-0040-0
    1. Mathematics — Study and teaching. 2. Mathematical ability —
Testing. I. Title. II. Series.
  QA11.K86 1994
  510'.7 — dc20   94-27372
                                        CIP

FIRST EDITION
PB Printing   10 9 8 7 6 5 4 3 2 1   *Code 94124*

Contents

Preface

The purpose of this book is to provide mathematics teachers and those who work with them a comprehensive and practical resource for planning and implementing alternative assessment in classrooms. The heavy emphasis on testing in American education, coupled with the tendency of reform efforts to emphasize thinking and problem solving, makes attention to alternative assessment a critical issue. Much of the attention to alternative assessment in mathematics has been at the national and state level, focused on developing items and instruments for large-scale assessments. Mathematics teachers and classrooms, although the target of this work, have not yet received the information or training that will enable them to implement new assessments. Just as important, very little attention has been given to the effects on teachers, their instructional practices, and their students' learning if they do use new approaches to evaluation. This book attempts to address these issues.

Mathematics teachers come from many different backgrounds, with a variety of experiences, mathematical knowledge, and levels of motivation to change their teaching and testing. This book is aimed at all of these teachers. The goal is to help them develop plans and ideas for implementing innovative assessment approaches in their mathematics classes. This is not a "how-to" book with specific answers or pages that can be copied and duplicated for students. It is a volume that presents ideas, questions, and examples of what works and what does not work in real classrooms. Readers should think about the book's implications for their own students. Much of the information requires synthesis and integration into the reader's unique setting. Some teachers are greatly constrained by the tests they use and the resources available to them. In spite of these constraints, the teachers with whom I have worked have found significant and useful ways to make alternative assessment help to improve their students' attitudes toward and learning of mathematics.

In addition to providing information and practical suggestions, the last part of the book contains summaries of assessment strategies tried out in the classroom. These descriptions provide the best information for other teachers. The variety of approaches that are effective in many types of school settings should give ideas that make sense to nearly everyone.

Acknowledgments

I would like to express my appreciation to the teachers who took part in the project on which much of this book is based. Their input, suggestions, and willingness to try new ideas were a continuing inspiration. Teachers like these give us hope that our schools and students are in good hands.

For their willingness during the past three years to do the million and one things that made my work easier, I would like to thank my students Dr. James Telese and Bonita McMullen.

The work on this book was funded in part by grants from the U.S. Department of Education and the Texas Education Agency. I appreciate this support; however, the opinions, findings, and conclusions or recommendations expressed are mine and do not necessarily reflect the views of these agencies.

I would like to thank the Jossey-Bass staff, especially Lesley Iura for her enthusiasm in publishing the book and Frank Welsch for his patient and insightful production work.

Most of all, I thank my wife Joan for her unwavering faith, support, and encouragement.

Bozeman, Montana   Gerald Kulm
August 1994

The Author

GERALD KULM is visiting professor and director of evaluation and assessment of the Systemic Teacher Excellence Preparation (STEP) project at Montana State University. He received his B.A. degree (1963) from Washington State University in mathematics, his M.A.T. degree (1967) from Cornell University in mathematics, and his Ed.D. degree (1971) from Columbia University Teachers College in mathematics education.

Kulm's main research, teaching, and administrative activities have been in mathematics attitudes, problem solving, assessment, and mathematics and science education policy. His experience includes work in directing mathematics and science education programs and projects at the American Association for the Advancement of Science. In 1976, he was selected as an Alexander von Humboldt Fellow and did research on mathematics problem solving at Bielefeld University in Germany. Kulm's edited books include *Assessing Higher Order Thinking in Mathematics* (1990) and *Science Assessment in the Service of Instruction* (1991, with S. Malcom).

Kulm was a member of the mathematics education faculty at Purdue University from 1971 to 1982, at the University of Kentucky from 1982 to 1984, and at Texas A&M University from 1990 to 1994.

To my loving wife and partner,
JOAN

MATHEMATICS
ASSESSMENT

Part One

BACKGROUND
AND PERSPECTIVES

Before considering the details of developing alternative assessment strategies that work in mathematics classrooms, it is necessary to create some perspectives on current goals and content for mathematics education. Mathematics is changing, both in its relationship to other disciplines and in the way it is taught from grade school to graduate school. The concern over how well American students are doing in mathematics has generated major national efforts to improve standards, instruction, and assessment. At the same time, knowledge about how students learn mathematics has changed. If teachers are to develop effective classroom assessment strategies, all of these factors must be taken into account. However, we must recognize the practical challenges that teachers face every day in their classrooms. It is not enough to make top-down policies and demand change. Practical strategies that are really effective must be available for implementation.

In Part One, we concentrate on the purposes and goals of assessment, with a focus on coming to an understanding of how these have changed and how these changes affect the classroom teacher. In Chapter One, the purposes and goals of mathematics assessment are discussed. This discussion includes a brief introduction to the National Council of Teachers of Mathematics (NCTM) *Curriculum and Evaluation Standards for School Mathematics,* which has provided specific areas for changed emphasis in mathematics content and the way it should be assessed. More recent ideas and standards from the NCTM *Assessment Standards for School Mathematics* are also reviewed. These documents are essential for developing a rational assessment plan that reflects the new directions in the mathematics teaching profession.

The important relationship between assessment and teaching is emphasized in Chapter Two. In the mathematics classroom, assessment is an essential tool used by the teacher to diagnose, monitor, and evaluate student progress. In recent years, mainly due to external pressures, the evaluation and comparison of achievement between groups of students, school

1

districts, states, and nations have become the central focus of assessment. This has caused a widened gap between instruction and assessment, leading to the unfortunate practice of "teaching to the test" — showing students how to take tests rather than how to think and solve problems. Alternative assessment offers a break from these practices, broadening and strengthening the relationship between mathematics teaching and evaluation.

An important shift in the field has arisen from the recognition that mathematical knowledge is constructed by the learner, built upon past experiences and connected to related ideas and concepts. In Chapters Three and Four, we discuss some key types of mathematical knowledge and ways to assess students' learning in these areas. It is now recognized that traditional testing has focused narrowly on mathematical skills and procedures, which are only one part of the knowledge necessary to use mathematics effectively. Without deep conceptual understanding and a knowledge of strategies for solving problems, the skills are inert and useless in real situations. A broad variety of assessment strategies must be used to monitor and provide feedback to teachers and students in order that active and interconnected mathematical knowledge can be constructed. More than anything else, this notion of multiple knowledge types and the assessment strategies relevant to them is a key perspective for understanding how to develop appropriate assessment programs.

1

PURPOSES AND
GOALS OF ASSESSMENT

WE ARE IN THE MIDST OF AN EDUCATIONAL REFORM MOVEMENT. THIS MOVEMENT involves reforming the reasons for and methods of assessing students (Kulm, 1990; Kulm & Malcom, 1991). Current testing is based on an assumption that no qualitative changes occur over time in the human mind or behavior, leading to the creation of "quick tests" that claim to handle two-year-olds and adults with the same format (Gardner, 1992). Other assumptions about testing are derived from the view that humans have inborn abilities. These assumptions lead to a paradigm in which individuals are tested (and schooled) in a uniform manner and students assessed according to predetermined norms. Tests have served as "gate keepers," allowing those who achieve best according to a prescribed norm to pass and failing those who might have creative or reflective approaches to addressing problems. A major goal of alternative assessment is to reveal individual strengths as well as areas that need further development.

Alternative assessments are being developed in nearly all curriculum areas. Gardner (1992) defines *assessment* as the obtaining of information about the skills and potentials of individuals, with dual goals of providing useful feedback to the individuals and helpful data to the surrounding community. Assessment elicits information in the course of ordinary performance. Teachers vary their instructional strategies because they understand that students have different learning styles. This natural experience and ability in good teaching can be incorporated into alternative assessment procedures for the students' benefit, identifying their strengths and weaknesses.

Goals of Classroom Mathematics Assessment

Alternative assessment provides opportunities to gain insight into students' broad knowledge and understanding of mathematics, not just skills and procedures. It furnishes better approaches to developing conceptual understanding and the relationships between procedures and concepts. Thus, a true reflection of students' mathematical knowledge can be identified. The primary purposes of assessment in the classroom are as follows:

- Improvement of instruction and learning
- Evaluation of student achievement and progress
- Feedback for the students, providing information to aid them in seeing inappropriate strategies, thinking, or habits
- Communication of standards and expectations
- Improvement of attitudes toward mathematics

The first two purposes are similar to the goals of traditional testing used by teachers and administrators. Good teachers try to use tests as a means for diagnosing their students' difficulties as well as monitoring their own instructional practices. Alternative assessment seeks to improve and expand teachers' instruction and evaluation of students through broader types of questions and multiple approaches.

Traditional tests, including many quizzes or end-of-chapter tests that are produced by textbooks, are designed with a narrow focus on a few specific skills, concepts, and procedures that have been covered. These assessments seldom give a broad picture of how well instruction has reached students of varying backgrounds and capabilities. It seems far too much to expect that published tests would have the capability to supply teachers with the type of information they need to improve or tailor their instruction to the needs of their own students. Consider, for example, the following assessment tasks:

Textbook question: Find the perimeter of a rectangle with a length of 8 meters and a width of 17 meters.

Alternative item: Susan wants to make a fence for her dog in the shape of a rectangle. She has 50 meters of fence. What are some sizes of rectangles that she could make? Which shape would be the best?

The textbook question provides feedback to the teacher as to whether the students have learned a procedure for finding the perimeter, given the lengths of two sides. The item does not assess students' understanding of a perimeter and does not get at the important ideas involving the relationship between perimeter and shape of a rectangle. A great majority of the students may correctly answer the textbook question, leading the teacher to an exaggerated estimate of their abilities. I have often had teachers express great dismay after giving an item like the dog-pen problem to students who they thought would do very well with it. The teachers' expectations were based on results from quizzes or tests made up of items like the textbook question.

All of them, upon seeing their students' performance on the open-ended item, resolve to change the way they teach the concept of perimeter.

These two types of question are also very different in the possibilities they provide for evaluations and grading of students' work. The textbook question has a right or wrong answer. Of course, one can see the steps the student uses in the procedure, and it is possible to note computational errors. But few opportunities exist to evaluate reasoning and communication skills, application of concepts to real applications, extended thinking, or the use of sophisticated or efficient solution strategies. All of these are possible using the alternative item.

Depending on a teacher's goals, the solution can be scored or graded holistically — on the overall solution and presentation of results. Or the teacher may wish to focus on the students' use of mathematical language or the reasoning used to find the "best" shape. Do the students recognize that a square-like rectangle provides the greatest area? Or do they use their knowledge about dog runs to develop rectangles that are longer and narrow? These options allow students to build on their own knowledge and experience and the teacher to evaluate the use of that knowledge. It is even possible to assess attitudes and habits of mind such as persistence, organization, and creativity.

The last three goals are also of great importance for alternative assessment. Traditional testing is limited in the information that can be provided to students about their strategies and thinking. It also sends clear signals to students that finding the correct answer, or becoming an expert "test taker," is important. Finally, test anxiety is perhaps the greatest factor in producing poor attitudes toward mathematics. Alternative assessments that offer a means for students to express and demonstrate mathematical ability in a variety of ways can reduce that anxiety and improve attitudes toward mathematics.

A great majority of mathematics teachers value problem solving, understanding, and application of mathematical skills as important objectives in school. But it is very difficult to teach these higher-order thinking abilities or to provide feedback and information to students about their thinking processes. The traditional approach is to try and teach specific skills such as "read the problem" or "assign a variable to the unknown." More recently, some teachers have encouraged students to make organized charts, to guess and check, or to break the problem into parts. Yet in the traditional testing paradigm, it is still the answer that counts. Students seldom receive feedback on the problem-solving strategies or processes that they use. And even if they do use an appropriate strategy, they only get credit for the correct answer. This does little to encourage students to learn problem-solving strategies.

Scoring protocols, keyed to open-ended tasks, can furnish the kind of information that students need to learn processes and to focus on understanding and meaning. For example, consider this scoring scheme for the solution of an open-ended problem:

> 3 points — Sensible method that leads to a correct solution. Clear procedures are used; there is awareness and use of relevant data and conditions; solution is complete, showing extended thought.
> 2 points — Method of solution is correct but there are some minor flaws and errors. Solution is not extended or generalized.
> 1 point — Incorrect process or major procedural errors. All data or conditions are not used.

This type of scoring rubric provides focused feedback to the student about the solution process. It emphasizes processes, procedures, and extended thought rather than only the correct answer. Other components of such a rubric could be constructed to provide a response to the students' presentation of the solution, use of graphic or symbolic representations, or other specific thinking and reasoning processes that are being taught.

The goal of communicating standards and expectations to students is a central concern to teachers and parents. One of the key ways that American students learn about expectations is through the tests they take in their classrooms, state assessment and standardized tests, and tests such as the SAT or ACT (which many students take as they complete their high school education). In the recent past, the message received by students has been that getting the correct answer is the main if not only goal. Many schools actually take class time or design special courses aimed at helping students pass state assessment exams or prepare for SAT tests. These activities send a very clear message that the test is more important than learning mathematics, thinking, and solving problems. There certainly are those who would argue that the test preparation process teaches students to think. That argument may have merit in some instances, but it is not the main goal of the test.

Alternative assessment approaches that include open-ended questions, presentation of solutions in both written and oral form, and other performances send very different messages to students about what is important in mathematics learning. The thinking and reasoning approaches and the way mathematical thoughts are presented can receive high marks even if the answer may not be complete or correct. The shift from an emphasis on producing correct answers to the expectation that students think and communicate is a major one for many students and teachers.

A final objective of alternative assessment involves the attitudes and beliefs about mathematics. More than any other aspect of mathematics, the anxiety and fear held by most people is a clear indictment of traditional testing approaches. The strong negative attitudes about mathematics is due to rote and abstract teaching approaches, compounded by tests that induce further anxiety. Traditional tests provide the opportunity to assess only a narrow range of student capability. Students who are visual thinkers, who are kinesthetically able, or who succeed best in a group setting are prevented from exhibiting their best performances in mathematics. Poor performances often lead to low self-esteem, anxiety, and avoidance. One of the most exciting aspects of alternative assessment strategies is that a large group of students who have been excluded from further work in mathematics-related fields can be successful.

Assessment and Mathematics Standards

New standards and assessments require more attention to problem solving. The National Council of Teachers of Mathematics has been at the forefront of developing standards for reforming education for all students. The 1989 *Curriculum and Evaluation Standards for School Mathematics* recommends more attention to problem solving and other forms of higher-order thinking in the assessment process. In late 1993, the NCTM released a working draft of a publication dealing directly with mathematics assessment, *Assessment Standards for School Mathematics*. *Assessment Standards* presents a vision that corresponds with the earlier ideas about curriculum and teaching presented in *Curriculum and Evaluation Standards* and in *Professional Standards for Teaching Mathematics* (1991). *Assessment Standards* also presents six standards for assessment, illustrates the use of these, and presents key questions regarding how classroom assessment practices can be changed. In the following discussion, we will present a summary of the main points of these two publications. The ideas and suggestions in this book are intended to provide concrete approaches that teachers can use in implementing both of these valuable NCTM publications.

The central goal of the NCTM *Curriculum and Evaluation Standards* is that students develop mathematical power. The kinds of abilities, attitudes, and habits of mind that characterize mathematical power are

- Application of knowledge to solve problems within mathematics and in other disciplines
- Use of mathematical language to communicate ideas
- Ability to reason and analyze
- Knowledge and understanding of mathematical concepts and procedures
- Positive disposition toward mathematics

Assessing mathematical power demands a change in the way we test students. To get an idea of how traditional and alternative assessment items might address mathematical power, consider the example items shown in Exhibits 1.1 and 1.2. How well does each item address the criteria for mathematical power?

Students completing the traditional test item must apply concepts and procedures and perhaps use reasoning and analytic abilities. There may be some question whether the item represents a "problem," since it seems more like a textbook example that may have been practiced. Communication skills and mathematical disposition are impossible to determine from a response to the traditional item.

Exhibit 1.1. Example of a Traditional Test Item.

A rectangular piece of land is to be used for a state park.

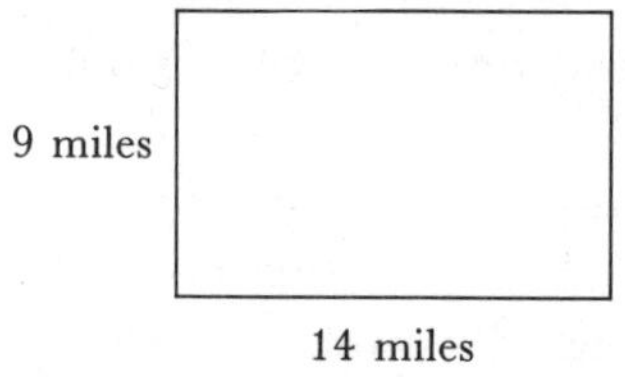

9 miles

14 miles

What is the perimeter of the piece of land?

A. 23 miles
B. 46 miles
C. 56 miles
D. 126 miles

Exhibit 1.2. Example of an Alternative Assessment Item.

A rock band has hired you to design the stage for the next concert. The stage should be rectangular and have an area of 1,000 square feet. It will have a security rope on both sides and the front. Make some drawings of different rectangles that have 1,000 square feet of area. How many feet of security rope is needed for each? Which shape would you use? Why?

The alternative item is open to a variety of solution approaches and strategies and to the application of procedures and concepts. Students are required to write and describe their solution, which not only evaluates mathematical communication abilities but also provides an opportunity to see their disposition toward the use of mathematics. Students assessed by this item receive a very different message about the use of the mathematics they are learning.

These two items illustrate the direction for assessment expressed by many mathematics educators. The NCTM *Standards* has summarized the kinds of things in assessment that should receive more emphasis and those that should be deemphasized.

Increased Emphasis	*Decreased Emphasis*
Evaluation of what students know and how they think	Evaluation of what students do not know
Assessment as an integral part of teaching and learning	Assessment as simply correct answers on a test to assign grades
Focus on a broad range of tasks and holistic view	Focus on a large number of isolated skills

Problem situations that require application of several ideas	Use of exercises or word problems that require only one or two skills
Use of multiple techniques, including written, oral, and demonstration	Use of only written tests
Use of calculators, computers, and manipulatives	Exclusion of calculators, computers, and manipulatives from all tests

Notice how many of the areas to receive increased emphasis are addressed in the alternative item about the rock band. This simple item builds on what students know and is relevant to them. Rather than applying a single procedure for finding perimeter, this item asks students to consider relationships between perimeter and area and to relate these to a real condition involving their judgment about the shape of the stage. The solution actually involves a variation on perimeter in which only two widths and a length are added to find the length of the rope. Communication skills are needed to explain why students chose particular dimensions for the stage.

Depending on how the teacher wishes to use the item, there are many opportunities to use manipulative materials, calculators, and other hands-on strategies. Students' work can be reported in many different modes, in addition to written solutions.

Assessment Standards

The National Council of Teachers of Mathematics has gone a step further in defining and discussing the role of assessment in mathematics education. The *Assessment Standards* working draft (1993) not only presents more detail about the nature of mathematics assessment but also reviews the related concerns of equity, validity, and consistency of assessment. Here are the six assessment standards presented in the working draft:

Standard 1:   Important Mathematics
Assessment should reflect the mathematics that is most important for students to learn.

Standard 2:   Enhanced Learning
Assessment should enhance mathematics learning.

Standard 3:   Equity
Assessment should promote equity by giving each student optimal opportunities to demonstrate mathematical power and by helping each student meet the profession's high expectations.

Standard 4:   Openness
All aspects of the mathematics assessment process should be open
to review and scrutiny.

Standard 5:   Valid Inferences
Evidence from assessment activities should yield valid inferences
about students' mathematics learning.

Standard 6:   Consistency
Every aspect of an assessment process should be consistent with
the purposes of the assessment [p. 27].

Although the standards are somewhat self-explanatory, the reader should
study them completely in order to understand their full meaning and implications. A great deal of the information in this book does help to explain how
the ideas in the *Assessment Standards* can be implemented in classrooms.

Some parts of the document are aimed at those who evaluate mathematics programs or set policy at district, state, and national levels. However, much of the information and many of the examples are relevant to
classroom teachers. The working draft sets out several purposes of assessment focused directly on teachers. For example, the document talks about
various purposes of assessment, including making instructional decisions,
monitoring student progress in the classroom, and using summative evaluations. Finally, the *Assessment Standards* raises some important issues — the
involvement of teachers in developing new assessments, the time and costs
involved, and the traditions of grading practices and tracking students.

As with other standards documents developed by the National Council of Teachers of Mathematics, once comments have been received from
mathematics teachers and others, this working draft will be revised and then
published as a final document. Based on the success of previous such documents, the *Assessment Standards* will most likely have a large impact on the
practice of mathematics evaluation, from local classrooms to national policy
directions. Meanwhile, for teachers who wish to develop and use effective
mathematics assessment, this book is very much in agreement with the ideas
and directions set forth by the working draft.

When alternative assessment is used properly, it eventually becomes
integral to instruction — no longer set off from the rest of classroom activity.
Until instruction and assessment approaches are aligned, there will be little
progress toward the goals of teaching problem solving and other types of
higher-order mathematical thinking. We can no longer tell students that problem solving and creativity are important but assess them with traditional
correct-answer tests. Alternative assessment techniques provide the opportunity to relate instructional goals to assessment and to make it possible for
that assessment to reinforce our teaching expectations. This approach has
the potential for developing higher-order thinking and reasoning abilities
in our students.

2

ASSESSMENT AND MATHEMATICS TEACHING

IN THINKING ABOUT TEACHING — WHETHER IT IS PLANNING, INSTRUCTION, OR evaluation — a key ingredient is what we know about our students. From a teacher's point of view, the main purpose of assessment should be to find out what we know, do not know, and might like to know about our students. After all, one of the central reasons for classroom assessment is to get information that will help improve teaching and learning. Types of information that might be useful to know about students include

- Demographics (age, gender, family background, ethnicity)
- Interests (academic, extracurricular)
- Abilities (academic, athletic, artistic, communication)
- Learning styles (analytic, impulsive, reflective, verbal, visual, cooperative)
- Motivation (academic, extrinsic, intrinsic, career)
- Attitude (mathematics, academic, general, self-esteem, confidence)
- Experiences (academic, travel, work)

Not all of these categories of information are mathematical, but they all are basic to learning mathematics. For example, interests that students have might open the way to abilities, motivation, or attitudes related to mathematics. Some information is obvious and objective. Other information can be based on beliefs about such things as race or gender that are open to bias or interpretation. Many teachers make assumptions about students based only on information from other teachers or on the students' behaviors in learning situations that are not designed to bring out their best. As teachers, we should rely on objective, consistent information about our students.

Alternative assessment items can provide a window not only into students' thinking and reasoning processes but also into their interests and attitudes, their general approach to solving problems, their experiences and background, and even their sense of humor. With a little insight, student

11

work can help us be better mathematics teachers. Consider the work of a seventh-grade student on an open-ended item in Figure 2.1.

Figure 2.1. Luke's Room.

Luke wants to paint one wall of his room. The wall is 20 feet wide and 8 feet high. It takes one can of paint to cover 80 square feet, and the paint is sold at $4.99 a can. What else does Luke need to think of? Make a plan for Luke's trip to the store for supplies for this painting job.

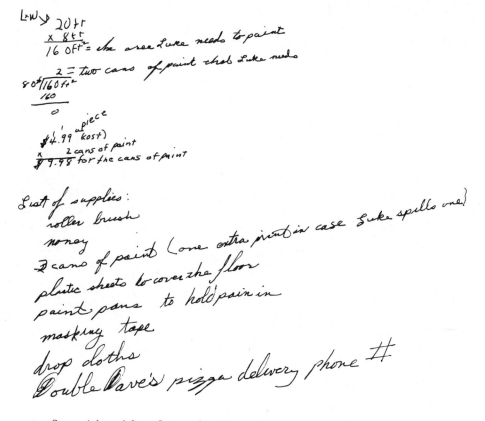

Source: Adapted from Stenmark, 1989, p. 16.

Let's do some speculating about this student. First, look at the work, and note some fairly obvious things:

- Handwriting
- Numbers that are labeled
- Computations
- Spelling and use of language

Does the handwriting suggest that this is a boy or girl? If so, why? The careful and complete labeling of all numbers indicates that the student has read the problem with comprehension, knows exactly what its conditions are, and has translated it accurately into its mathematical representations. The numbers have meaning, rather than simply being values that are combined without meaning or understanding. The computations are done efficiently and correctly, using the common algorithms usually taught in school. The student can obviously apply algorithmic knowledge to a nonroutine problem. The words are spelled correctly; the name of the pizza delivery is capitalized as a proper name. Even though the problem does not call for written sentences or explanations, the student has used extended responses to provide information and reasons for some answers.

Now consider some more subtle aspects of the solution:

- Scientific-style labeling of square feet
- Use of the equal sign in the answers to calculations
- Allowance of the extra can of paint
- Use of specialized vocabulary such as "drop cloth" and "masking tape"
- Inclusion of the phone number for a local pizza delivery store

The precision and careful use of labeling, the length-by-width sidenote for the calculation of area, and the use of equal signs to express answers all point to abilities in mathematical knowledge and reasoning. The knowledge appears to be well integrated, rather than consisting of unconnected, memorized bits and pieces. This student shows a readiness and ability to proceed into the study of algebra and the use of mathematics to model real-world situations.

The specialized vocabulary related to painting suggests that the student may have either helped or observed someone who did similar types of work, perhaps at home. The student may have visited hardware or paint stores, observing the types of supplies needed. The list shows attention to detail and the ability to plan ahead and anticipate difficulties.

Finally, the degree of completeness in the solution provides some insight into the student's attitudes, habits of mind, and disposition toward mathematics. The NCTM *Standards* stresses the importance of students' developing self-confidence in their abilities as a part of gaining mathematical power. A student who includes a pizza phone number in the solution to a mathematics problem appears both to be confident and to possess a certain sense of humor and joy in doing mathematics.

This analysis of a simple nonroutine problem for a single student is probably far more comprehensive than many teachers would do in an assessment or test. But many aspects of the student can be seen informally by the insightful teacher in the course of using an efficient scoring scheme while grading the work. The main point is that this type of assessment task creates the possibility, whether formally or informally, for a teacher to see a wide range of abilities, skills, and attitudes. If more traditional tests are used exclusively, many characteristics of students can go unnoticed and unappreciated.

Background Information About Students

Objective observation can tell us some things about students. We can see how they look, how they dress, whether they are boys or girls, or whether they are tall or short. There is a great deal of other information that we think we know or that we believe. For example, if the second child from a family is in our class, we may mistakenly assume some abilities or interests based on experience with the older sibling. Teachers may base expectations on the fact that they have "had a student like that before," that the student lives in a particular part of town, or that he or she has parents with a certain type of job. These kinds of subjective observations and judgments are not appropriate and can greatly interfere with good teaching.

Nevertheless, valid and useful subjective judgments are made and used constantly. Daily observations can lead us to predict behavior that will happen again tomorrow. Judgments based on direct evidence can provide important information about students. An essential part of assessment is to go beyond correct or incorrect answers and beyond test scores and grades. Assessment should provide approaches to finding information that can broaden our ideas about what students know and are able to do.

One view of information is that the more we know about our students, the better we might be able to adjust our teaching so that it more effectively increases students' interest and comprehension. At the same time, information about students might lead to preconceptions about their ability or motivation. Teacher expectations are a powerful influence on learning. If after reviewing standardized test scores and previous grades, a teacher believes that a student cannot excel, the chances are that she or he will not do well.

Schools and teachers use information they have collected to place students in tracks; this has a lifelong effect. Studies indicate, for example, that 84 percent of seventh graders are placed in ability groups in mathematics (Useem, 1991). These placements, based on previous grades and tests, determine the courses that students will take throughout high school and beyond. How can we be sure that our tests and grades are so valid that they should have such enduring effects on students? The second International Achievement Study (McKnight et al., 1987) found that only in the United States and Canada did students' mathematical scores relate to the type of mathematics class in which they were placed. No other information about students was so significant as whether he or she was enrolled in an advanced, general, or remedial mathematics class.

Decisions about students and their future in mathematics are part of the responsibility of teachers. It is therefore imperative that we have the broadest and richest information possible about student achievement. Rather than producing a few numbers or grades, assessments should yield profiles, descriptive information, interests, attitudes, and other information that can provide a clear picture of abilities and aptitudes.

Information About Students' Mathematical Thinking

In Chapters Three and Four, a complete discussion of types of mathematical knowledge will be provided. In this section, students' knowledge of procedures and concepts will be used to illustrate the range and depth of information a teacher needs to know about mathematical thinking. Current tests often furnish information primarily on the procedures that students are able to do correctly. There are many other more important ideas that students should know about procedures than simply how to perform them. The NCTM *Standards,* for example, suggests that students should know things such as recognizing when to use a particular procedure. Research studies indicate that the primary strategy many students use in choosing a procedure for solving word problems is to look at the relative sizes of the numbers. If the numbers are about the same size, students will add or subtract. If one number is significantly larger than the other, students multiply or divide. Other students use key words. They look for *of* or *and* as a clue to choosing an operation.

Other important aspects of mathematical thinking include being able to justify the steps taken in carrying out a procedure, recognizing an incorrect procedure, and generating original procedures. Teachers often ask students to show all of their work and to check their solutions. Yet traditional test items seldom focus specifically on this skill. Alternative assessment tasks can be used not only to determine students' ability to justify steps but to send a message about the importance of this knowledge. Look at this item:

> Maria is helping her younger brother do his math. He wants to know why you change the 3 to a 4 and drop the 7 when rounding 5.37 to the nearest tenth. How can Maria explain this to her brother?

This item goes beyond a rote rule or reason such as "round up if the number is larger than four." Students should know that the justification is more than simply stating the rule for carrying out the procedure. Justification of steps in procedures often requires an understanding both of the procedure itself and of the underlying concepts and prerequisites as well. In this case, the student must know that 0.37 is between 0.30 and 0.40 and also that it is closer to 0.40. Further, this knowledge must be connected to the concept of rounding in order to give meaning and justification to the rule. Although it is not possible or necessary to assess this depth of understanding on each and every procedure, students should be able to justify the important procedural skills they learn.

Recognition of incorrect procedures is becoming an increasingly important part of procedural knowledge. The use of calculators and computers will continue to remove the burden of carrying out computations for many of the procedures that have been drilled and practiced. However, pushing calculator buttons and writing or selecting computer programs place a heavy emphasis on recognizing the correct procedure to be used and on knowing when an incorrect procedure has been suggested or applied. This knowledge can be emphasized, taught, and assessed from the very early grades onward. Consider this item:

> Bill says that an increase from 10 to 40 is a 300% increase, and that means a decrease from 40 to 10 must be a 300% decrease. Explain what is wrong with Bill's reasoning.

This type of item gauges students' understanding of an important concept involved in percentages that is difficult and often misunderstood. The item focuses directly on communicating to students that it is important to understand the underlying concept, rather than trying to memorize rules such as "a percent decrease can never be greater than 100."

The ability to generate new procedures is often overlooked and very often discouraged in traditional instruction. Yet few real-world problems occur in such simple forms that standard algorithms can be applied. For example, in determining the amount of lawn food for a yard, one can seldom simply find the area of a rectangle. Often, different shapes must be pieced together and estimates used. Preschool children seem to invent new procedures naturally. They often generate approaches for adding numbers. For example, to add five and seven, they might know that five plus five equals ten, then simply count up two more to twelve. Current tests do not reveal this type of mathematical thinking. In fact, if the test is timed, a student who thinks this way may not finish some items; a teacher may conclude that the student is deficient in mathematical understanding. It is important that students' ideas about mathematical procedures are not formalized too early and too narrowly, resulting in the attitude that there is only one way to find a solution and that the correct procedure can only be learned from a book or a teacher.

Think about your students. What procedures are you confident they really know, beyond just being able correctly to execute and carry out the steps? Could they give some reasons for these steps? Could they understand when a procedure was applied inappropriately? Could they recognize if another student did the procedure correctly or incorrectly? Do they know its limitations? Do they appreciate the power and efficiency of certain procedures, such as the ones used to find the greatest common denominator, to find the roots of a quadratic equation, or to simplify a fraction? Knowledge of procedures goes far beyond simply performing them quickly and correctly. The NCTM *Standards* and other recommendations stress that mathematics teaching in the future will move away from "covering" and memorizing procedures that are marginally useful and move toward an emphasis on the deeper understanding of key procedures and the ability to justify and modify them for application to more advanced concepts and real situations.

A second major area of mathematical learning is conceptual knowledge. Concepts in mathematics are the foundation for understanding procedures and for problem solving. An early understanding of a concept is broadened and enriched with each experience a child has with it. Students can develop misconceptions if they are required to use concepts in new contexts without sufficient experience or hands-on practice. For instance, because most examples of triangles they have seen happen to be acute, students may assume that all triangles are acute. Learning and assessment tasks that are limited in context and application can result in poor understanding or limited conceptualization.

Again, think about your own students. What concepts do they know? What concepts are you not so sure they know? If your students know the concept of a triangle, for example, they should be able to define it verbally, identify and label its parts, draw or make a model, give examples of various types, and identify figures that are not triangles. They should be able to compare the triangle with other figures and to communicate orally, in writing, and symbolically about their understanding. The item shown in Figure 2.2 can assess some of these abilities.

Figure 2.2. Understanding the Triangle.

Give as many similarities and differences about these figures as you can. Draw a figure that is like Figure A. Explain why it is like Figure A.

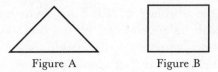

Figure A   Figure B

This item provides the opportunity to assess a student's use of terminology and mathematical language. It also offers a chance to use concepts such as sides, lengths, angles, triangles, and quadrilaterals to describe and differentiate between the figures. Finally, the item allows the teacher to see a student's performance in drawing a triangle and using the concept of triangle to differentiate it from the other one.

Merely stating a definition or identifying an example of a concept is not a sufficient assessment of understanding. In fact, most students learn concepts best by working with models, drawings, and applications rather than by starting with a definition. Since concepts are formed over time and consist of complex networks of connections among other concepts, facts, and principles, assessment must be sensitive enough to account for this development.

In order to teach mathematics effectively, we must understand how our students think. Traditional testing can tell us mainly what students know and the skills they have developed. Alternative assessments are needed to help us see the development of mathematical knowledge and a complete picture of students' thinking and reasoning abilities.

3

PROCEDURAL AND
CONCEPTUAL LEARNING

ONE OF THE REAL CHALLENGES OF TEACHING MATHEMATICS IS TO FIND A PROPER balance between conceptual understanding and procedural skills. Without a sound understanding of concepts, skills may be used mechanically and easily forgotten. At the same time, strong mathematical skills and computation can help students build understanding of new concepts. So it is not an either-or situation. But learning mathematical concepts and procedures is not an end in itself. Their application in solving problems and learning new mathematics is the ultimate goal for our students.

Given the difficult balance of conceptual understanding and mathematical skills, testing adds a further complication. It seems easy to test skills. Many teachers also believe that if students demonstrate skills, they must understand the underlying concepts; and if students cannot do the skills, they cannot be expected to understand concepts and cannot progress to higher-level course work. As we saw earlier, the result is that many teachers create a vicious cycle that ends in students being tracked into increasingly lower-level classes, which repeat the same skills "drill and kill" year after year. How can we break this cycle and build understanding as well as skills? Alternative approaches to testing and assessment provide one answer.

Types of Mathematical Knowledge

In order to think about designing assessment approaches, we need to develop a clear idea of the characteristics of different types of mathematical knowledge. Even this task should be undertaken cautiously. It is not easy to categorize or separate types of mathematical knowledge. For example, we can think about the concept of addition and also realize that there are procedures for addition. With this caveat in mind, the following paragraphs outline the definitions currently used by mathematics educators to talk about different types of knowledge.

Procedural knowledge is often identified with mathematical skills. What is the definition of a *skill*? Bell, Costello, & Kuchemann (1983) believe that the term cannot be restricted to computational procedures of arithmetic and algebra. It includes any well-established, multistep procedure that may involve symbolic expression, geometrical figures, or any other mathematical representation. For instance, moving the decimal point to the right one place when multiplying a decimal number by ten is a skill. A key feature of a skill is that it involves an action or a transformation. Carpenter (1986) uses *skill* to mean procedural knowledge, a step-by-step procedure executed in a specific sequence.

According to Bell et al. (1983), there are two kinds of concepts: (1) a thing such as a rhombus or fraction that requires a definition and (2) a relationship expressed as a statement, such as "multiplication of real numbers is commutative." The first type of concept may be defined extensively by providing examples and nonexamples or intensively by stating defining properties. A conceptual structure consists of a network of concepts and relationships, which some researchers call a schema. These structures support the selection and performance of procedures and enable the problem solver to adapt a procedure to a new situation. When a new concept or relationship is learned, another node or link is formed in the existing cognitive structure. Carpenter (1986) defines *conceptual knowledge* as that which consists of a rich network of relationships between pieces of information and that permits flexibility in accessing and using the information.

Traditional testing places heavy emphasis on procedural knowledge and on the vocabulary of concepts. One consequence of this emphasis is impoverished conceptual knowledge and weak or nonexistent links between procedural and conceptual knowledge. This linking of the two types of knowledge is a bidirectional process. Without the connection to conceptual knowledge, children acquire flawed or narrowly memorized procedural knowledge. Learning must be continually analyzed during teaching, so that instruction can be carefully designed to allow the development of conceptual knowledge and its link to procedural knowledge.

Assessing Procedural Knowledge

We have always assumed that procedural knowledge is easiest to observe and test. Since much of the mathematics that children learn in school has a characteristic of procedural linearity, traditional instruction and testing have focused on this aspect, rather than on the complex relationships involved in the schema of conceptual knowledge or the unseen processes used in strategic thinking.

We have often assumed that if a student has learned a procedure, the related conceptual knowledge has also been acquired. Most classroom tests and many standardized tests include only procedural items. Students are sometimes asked to identify a concept vocabulary term, such as *triangle* or *polynomial.* Of course, it is clear that many students have learned procedural skills without understanding why the procedure works or what the underlying concepts mean. Students can also memorize vocabulary terms or match words to the appropriate picture without being able to use the concept in a problem.

This is not to imply that procedural knowledge is not important. On the one hand, it is imperative that students be able to perform key procedures easily and flexibly. On the other, procedures should be built on related conceptual knowledge rather than performed from rote memory. Our students should be aware of the limits procedures have and should know when to draw on conceptual knowledge in order to apply the appropriate procedure to solve a problem. These aspects of procedural and conceptual knowledge require some alternative assessment approaches that go beyond determining correct and incorrect answers to simple computational exercises.

Figure 3.1 presents some assessment tasks that not only test students' knowledge of procedures but also supply information about conceptual links. Two or three important characteristics are illustrated by these items. Most of the time, procedures are taught as if they must be done exactly the same way by everyone. There can be so much emphasis on form and format that children lose sight of the idea that procedures are useful for answering questions. These items can determine whether students can actually perform procedures but are open enough to allow them to determine which procedure to use and when.

Figure 3.1. Alternative Procedure Assessment.

Item 1. Find two whole numbers greater than 10 whose product is 726.

Item 2. The five numbers 1, 2, 3, 4, and 5 are placed in the boxes to form a multiplication problem. If they are placed to give a maximum product, the product will fall between:

a. 10,000 and 22,000   b. 22,001 and 22,300
c. 22,301 and 22,400   d. 22,401 and 22,500

Item 3. Your cousin is just beginning to learn more about numbers. She doesn't understand what $4 \times 3 = 12$ means. How would you explain this to her? You may use pictures or graphs.

Item 4. You just got a new puppy. A friend gave you $10.00 to spend on your puppy. You decide to buy a collar, a dish, and a toy. The chart shows the prices at three different stores.

	Acme	Pet World	Top Pet
collar	$3.50	$3.00	$4.00
dish	$4.25	$4.00	$4.50
toy	$2.75	$2.25	$2.50

a. Choose a possible selection of collar, dish, and toy that you could buy. What is the cost? How much change would you receive?
b. How many different ways could you buy the three items and still spend $10 or less? Show each combination.

An important message that these items send is that there may be more than one answer to a question or problem. Most often, students learn procedures aimed at finding an exact answer. They do not have experience with the idea that there are procedures, such as estimation, that may have more than one answer, depending on who is answering the question or its purpose. A second important component of procedural knowledge is an understanding of why it works. Although most teachers probably agree that this is important, few include it on assessments. We sometimes assume that if a student practices a procedure enough, the understanding will gradually just happen. In Figure 3.1, Item 3 provides an example of one way this knowledge can be assessed.

Estimation is becoming a very important skill as connected to computational procedures and as a procedure itself. Students must know a variety of estimation procedures, when to apply them, and why they work. Items 1 and 2 provide two examples for assessing estimation. In Item 2, an estimate is clearly being asked for. In Item 1, estimation is a good strategy to use in getting started on the question, in determining about how large the two numbers might be. In Item 4, estimation can be used to get a general idea of whether the cost is less than $10.

Finally, no discussion of procedures would be complete without considering the use of calculators or computers. Note that calculators could be used in any or all of the four sample items but differently in each one. In Items 1 and 2, the calculator could be a direct computational aid, making it possible for the student to concentrate on solving the problem. In Item 4, a calculator could be used to check or verify a computation. In Item 3, the student may not use the calculator, but one could imagine ways it could be used in the explanation.

These tasks are clearly different from the traditional items usually found on tests of computational skills. In many state and national assessments, purely computational items are no longer used to assess this skill. We have learned that being able to do a computation does not mean a student can apply it, even in the simplest of word problems. New teaching and assessment approaches must broaden the use of procedural knowledge to include applications and understanding of why procedures work and how they are applied.

Assessing Conceptual Knowledge

Traditional approaches to testing conceptual knowledge have included evaluating whether students can define a concept, show or choose an example of one, or discriminate among concepts. But there is much more to understanding concepts than this. Students should also be able to generate examples of what these are — as well as are not. Students should be able to compare differences between concepts and to recognize different interpretations. They should be able to translate, from written to symbolic to graphic to verbal, descriptions or representations of concepts.

All of these abilities related to conceptual knowledge are important for applying concepts, for understanding how procedures work, and for reasoning and problem solving. This deep conceptual understanding is also essential for being able to communicate mathematical knowledge effectively. Of course, new and nontraditional approaches to assessment are needed when we require and expect students to understand in this broader and deeper way.

In Figure 3.2, we see some assessment tasks that not only test students' conceptual knowledge but also provide information about links to procedural knowledge and to the application of concepts to reasoning and problem solving. Each of the items in Figure 3.2 requires much more than just defining or identifying a concept. In Item 1, the concept of place value must be understood and applied in the explanation. Actually, the term *place value* is not used in the question, making it possible to assess understanding of the concept, rather than the vocabulary itself. Students often actually do understand a concept, even though they may not have connected it to the word.

Items 2 and 4 require a student to generate further examples or representations of concepts. Students may have only a single image of concepts such as fractions and geometric figures. For example, they may think of one-half only in terms of a semicircle, since "pies" may be the only representation for the concept that has been used by the teacher or textbook. In order to understand and be able to apply concepts fully, items such as this must be used to allow a broader range of representations. Similarly, Item 4 illustrates a very common difficulty that students have with the concept of area. Formal-level thinking requires the ability to know that different shapes can have the same area. An item that asks the student to generate some different shapes provides an assessment of performance, rather than simply computing area. Item 4 also makes connections between several concepts, including coordinates of points, vertices, origin, and measurement.

Item 3 gets directly at the ability to compare and contrast figures. This type of item is superior to more traditional items that just ask students to name figures or to choose which one matches a given definition or set of criteria. The student must concentrate on the important characteristics in order to generate the differences and similarities. A follow-up question could ask the student which of the differences are important. For example, does it matter if the figures are different colors or if one is "right side up" and the other is "upside down"? These open-ended questions can be used to evaluate the connections that students have made in understanding concepts.

Procedural knowledge and language facility are integral to concept development. By encouraging and eliciting classroom discussion about concepts, teachers can help students to build their mathematical communication skills and also facilitate the connections necessary for understanding. In a similar way, encouraging discussions about procedures can accomplish the dual goals of eliciting the underlying conceptual bases for procedures and developing communication ability while simultaneously developing students'

Figure 3.2. Alternate Conceptual Assessment.

Item 1. A visitor from outer space has just arrived. The visitor is confused about our number system and has asked you, "Is 5 plus 29 equal to 529?" Answer the visitor's question, and explain your answer.

Item 2. Use the figure below to show $\frac{1}{2}$ in as many ways as you can. You may draw more figures if necessary. For each way you find, explain how you know you have $\frac{1}{2}$.

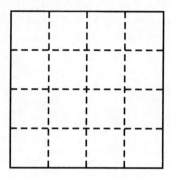

Item 3. Tell everything you can think of about the similarities and differences between these two figures.

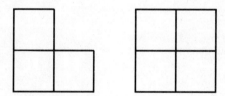

Item 4. The origin, 0, and point A on this graph represent opposite vertices of a rectangle whose area is 24 square inches.

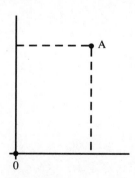

a. Give one set of possible coordinates of point A.

b. Keep one vertex at the origin and the opposite vertex in the first quadrant. Mark and label the coordinates of at least two more points that could be opposite vertices of rectangles of area 24 square inches. Explain why you chose these coordinates.

procedural skills. The important connections among procedures, concepts, and communication imply that the assessment of procedural knowledge should go beyond asking students to carry out an algorithm: test items should include opportunities to reason and explain how and why a procedure works.

Teaching and assessment of concepts and procedures ought to be integrated. Concepts can be taught using examples, as well as nonexamples; differences between concepts and different interpretations can also be identified. Throughout these activities, students are involved, allowing the teacher to assess their understanding at a deeper and broader level. This approach to teaching concepts is an example of how instruction can be integrated with assessment.

4

PROBLEM SOLVING AND STRATEGIC KNOWLEDGE

THE PRIMARY REASON FOR CHANGING THE DIRECTION OF ASSESSMENT HAS BEEN to focus on problem solving as a key part of the mathematics curriculum. Continued efforts are aimed at moving beyond simple word problems toward evaluating the processes that students should learn and use in a variety of situations. In *How to Solve It,* Polya (1957) provides a summary of processes for understanding the problem, planning, carrying out the solution, and looking back at the solution. That these processes are reflected in the NCTM *Standards* suggests that the assessment of problem solving should include looking at whether students can formulate problems, apply a variety of strategies, verify and interpret results, and generalize solutions. In this chapter, we will look at some specific examples of approaches to assessing problem-solving processes.

In recent work on mathematical thinking, attention has been given to the notion that people have strategies that guide their choice of what skills to use or what knowledge to draw upon during the course of problem solving, investigation, or verification of a discovery. In other words, these are "superprocedures" or programs that operate on the other types of knowledge (Bell et al., 1983). Sometimes, the term *metacognition* is used to describe this kind of thinking. In addition to providing the decision-making processes during problem solving, strategic knowledge also consists of general and specific approaches to planning and carrying out the steps in solving the problem. Strategic knowledge is included in the definition of *mathematical power,* a key focus of the NCTM *Standards:*

> This term [mathematical power] denotes an individual's abilities to explore, conjecture, and reason effectively to solve non-routine problems. This notion is based on the recognition of mathematics as more than a collection of concepts and skills to be mastered; it includes methods of investigating and reasoning,

means of communication, and notions of context. In addition, for each individual, mathematical power involves the development of personal self-confidence [1989, p. 5].

In traditional instruction and testing, strategic knowledge is integrated within the examples provided by the teacher and the questions or problems asked of the student. Very seldom is the student taught specific strategies that work, and less often are students tested on their knowledge of problem-solving strategies. Only a few students are able to acquire strategic knowledge on their own in this way. Even the more able students are unlikely to learn strategies if they are not provided open-ended or nonroutine problems to solve. Strategic knowledge must be explicitly taught, modeled, and practiced. Furthermore, it should be assessed, just as skills and concepts are tested.

Direct assessment of strategic knowledge also requires specific approaches. It is not sufficient to provide problems and determine whether the answer is correct. The processes and strategies themselves must be the objects of assessment. The line of reasoning and the types of decision making used by the student must be a part of the evaluation.

An Example Problem

As an illustration of some of the ideas and issues involved in assessing problem-solving strategies, we will look in detail at the solution to a nonroutine problem by real students. In Chapter Two, we examined one student's solution to this problem and discovered that through an insightful analysis of a written solution, a great deal could be learned about the person's mathematical knowledge, thinking and reasoning skills, and attitudes and beliefs. Here we look at how a group of eighth-grade students worked together in solving the problem. Once again, an analysis of the solution will help to illustrate some ideas about problem solving.

> Luke wants to paint one wall of his room. The wall is 20 feet wide and 8 feet high. It takes one can of paint to cover 80 square feet, and the paint is sold at $4.99 a can. What else does Luke need to think of? Make a plan for Luke's trip to the store for supplies for this painting job.

Here are some excerpts from a taped discussion of the students' solution:

Boy: We need to figure out how many cans of paint.

Boy: The wall is 20 feet tall, wide. No, it's 20 feet wide.

Boy: So, it is 160 feet.

Girl: 160 feet? Two cans of paint.

Boy: Two cans of paint.

Boy: That would be 160, two feet.

Boy: The paint cans are $4.99 apiece, so it's eight, nine, $4.99.

Girl: All right, if we have 160 and two cans of paint . . .

Boy: It's $9.98!

At this point, it seems that the problem was understood, and there is a good start in arriving at a solution. If traditional approaches to assessment were being used, the correct answer of $9.98 would receive full credit. But this item asks for a plan. In fact, it does not even ask the students to find the cost of the paint. They have assumed on their own that this is important to calculate. The requirement to do more than calculate reveals some other insights into the students' problem-solving abilities. Look at the continued discussion:

Boy: You only have to paint one wall of his room. It's 20 by 8, and that whole wall space is 120 feet.

Girl: So that's 20 by 8, so that's multiplication.

Girl: Yes.

Boy: Sixty times 60.

Girl: Twenty times 8 and then times 2 because we've got to find the other two walls.

Boy: No, no, he only paints one room; he only paints one wall.

Girl: Well, how do we know which wall?

Boy: Well, they just gave you the measurements of it.

Girl: But there's one wall, and it's 20.

Boy: No, we're only painting one wall, though.

Girl: So we are painting this wall right here, this 8-feet-high wall?

Boy: No, the wall is, say, this is the wall; it's 8 feet this way and 20 feet up. But to find the area, we have to find the area, which is 120.

Girl: Length times width.

Boy: But, which we did.

Girl: If you take 20 times 8, that equals 160, and if you multiply it by 2, 2 more, that's 320.

Girl: Yeah, we don't need to do that if we find the area. That's perimeter.

Boy: Area?

Girl: So he needs two?

Boy: Two paint cans because each one covers 80 square feet, which is $9.98.

Girl: So you need to take $10.00 to the store.

Boy: Right.

This exchange reveals that there wasn't so clear an understanding as it seemed. The students clarify the conditions of the problem to reaffirm the dimensions and the fact that there is one wall. They also review the concepts of area and perimeter and the appropriate formula to find area.

In the next segment, the students begin to connect the problem to real life. It becomes clear that the work they have been doing so far is much like a typical textbook word problem. The attitude shifts somewhat as they begin to take the problem into a real context:

Girl: Take $10.00 . . .

Boy: But we have to figure out tax!

Boy: There is no tax!

Boy: It's 8 percent.

Boy: We don't know that. It could be 20 percent!

Boy: In real life it's 8 percent.

Girl: It doesn't say we have to figure tax.

Boy: But these are real-life problems.

Girl: Yeah, but we don't have to figure tax.

Girl: Why don't we do two answers, one with tax and one without it.

Boy: What's 8 percent of $10.00? Those aren't percentage signs.

Girl: It probably doesn't have one, so maybe we're going to have to figure out percentage.

Boy: You could put it, 8 percent, 8 percent of 10 is probably about $1.25 out of $9.98.

Girl: So why don't we do that then?

Boy: OK. Oh, we have to guess and check! What is the 8 percent of, say, 10, rounded?

Girl: Eight percent of 10?

Girl: So what else is it we need? OK, so we really have the first part of the question. You take $10.00, and we get what, $.02 back? Is that right?

Boy: Yeah. But with tax you have to buy it. Would it be best to take about $12.00, just to be safe? Because with tax on $9.00, it won't be more than $2.00. That way you would have about $1.50 extra.

Girl: But it doesn't say he has to pay for tax.

Boy: But it's a real-life problem.

Now we can see how important a student's perceptions and beliefs about problems are in the solution process. One student feels that unless a question is explicitly posed, there is no need to answer it. Another student tries to relate the problem to his own experience, knowing that the local tax is 8 percent. Notice that they do not find the amount of tax but agree to bring more than enough money to cover it. It is interesting that as the thinking shifts from specific data to more open-ended and fuzzy questions, the numerical values become less precise. Whereas a figure such as $9.98 made sense earlier, the solution to 8 percent of $9.98 is something less than $2.00. The students next consider further needs for the job:

Girl: What else does he need that you can think of?

Boy: Nothing.

Girl: Wouldn't he need brushes? To paint the walls?

Boy: Brushes! Rollers.

Girl: What about some overalls to paint in?

Girl: Really, so he won't get his other clothes dirty.

Boy: It's true.

Boy: Like a tablecloth?

Girl: Why does he need a tablecloth?

Boy: To wear.

Boy: To cover up his furniture.

Girl: Why don't we just buy him an apron?

Girl: Something kind of like sheets and stuff to cover up his furniture.

Boy: A roller is about $6.00. So we need one roller.

Girl: We need a brush at least.

Boy: Roller, $6.00.

Girl: Tablecloth and sheets. I guess he probably already has sheets at home.

Girl: What about an apron?

Girl: What does he need an apron for?

Boy: To cover his clothing up so he can paint.

Girl: He can take an apron with pockets to stick his paint brushes in.

Boy: We need to get an apron.

Boy: How much does a roller cost? About $6.00?

Girl: Kevin, we don't know.

Boy: Well, we need to guess.

Girl: We have to make a chart of this.

Boy: We need to guess.

Boy: Aren't we supposed to finish the problem?

Girl: It says make a plan for Luke's trip to the store for supplies for this painting job. It doesn't say that we need to figure out . . .

Boy: It doesn't say, but it would be good to do. You don't do something just because you don't say to.

Boy: Then a roller costs $4.50.

Girl: How about $5.00?

Girl: Brush. Somewhere in the neighborhood of like . . .

Boy: $2.25.

Boy: Two to three dollars.

Boy: OK, an apron. You can go down to Woolworth's. At Woolworth's, $3.50?

Girl: You can go to the Dollar Store and get an apron for a dollar.

Girl: Everything's a dollar.

Boy: But it has to have pockets.

Girl: They have, like, cooking aprons.

Boy: Yeah. OK. We need to add that into the money. Say $12.00 with tax plus $5.00 is $17.00 plus the $2.50 . . .

Girl: We have $11.50 right here so we could just round that. We could put $13.00 and then that way . . .

Boy: That would cover the tax.

Girl: Yeah, if there was tax.

Boy: If it's not food, it has to be taxed.

Girl: So let's just have $13.00 and $10.00 is $23.00. So that's about how much he needs.

Boy: It would be good just to add a dollar, just in case the tax went up.

Girl: Twenty-five dollars. How about that?

Boy: Yeah, $25.00; that's a good number. You could bring a twenty and a five.

Girl: We came out with $25.00?

Boy: In all.

In this part of the solution process, the students seem to come the closest yet to considering the entire situation and to using their real experiences along with problem-solving strategies. In considering supplies, a certain creativity and imagination are applied. As they try to develop a total budget, they use estimation skills, rounding, and mental computation. They also are aware of strategies such as guessing and making a chart or list. It is interesting that their main focus continues to be arriving at a final dollar amount for the supplies. A shopping list of supplies does not appear to be a viable solution. Their experience with mathematical problem solving has taught them that a numerical solution is expected.

Assessment of Solution Processes

Using this example, what can we say about assessment of these students and their solution processes and strategies? There is certainly more to think about than whether they are good or poor problem solvers or even whether their grade should be an A, B, or C. The difficulty in assessing solution processes is in choosing what to evaluate. The focus of the assessment will very quickly send messages to the student about what is valued. Notice that in this solution the students discussed what they thought was expected of them several times.

One approach is to look specifically at the solution process, using a framework such as Polya's as a guide. How well did the students understand the problem? Was there evidence that they planned the approach? Was the solution correct and reasonable, and were the steps along the way correct? Did they check or generalize the solution, or determine whether it satisfied the conditions of the problem? Many teachers use an outline such as this to assign points to each part of the solution process. For example, a student may receive a three out of four for understanding the problem or a two out of four for planning. These scores help students to focus their work on specific problem-solving processes. A more detailed discussion of scoring will be given in Chapter Ten.

My discussion of the solution process provides an example of some analysis that might be done. For example, these students were able to come to a good understanding of the mathematical relationships in this problem, but they did not have a good estimate of a simple percentage. They seemed to have a narrow idea of what a solution to this type of problem should look like. Their final figure of $25.00 was accepted without doing a great deal of looking back and considering if it made sense.

Another way of looking at assessment is to consider a broad definition of problem solving, such as that contained in the NCTM *Standards* (1989, p. 75), which expects students to be able to

- Use problem-solving approaches to investigate and understand mathematical content
- Formulate problems from situations within and outside mathematics
- Develop and apply a variety of strategies to solve problems, with emphasis on multistep and nonroutine problems
- Verify and interpret results with respect to the original problem situation
- Generalize solutions and strategies to new problem situations
- Acquire confidence in using mathematics meaningfully

This set of criteria might be used to assess a collection or portfolio of students' work in problem solving. A single problem would clearly not suffice. The example we have been looking at could be employed to assess students' progress on the last four of these criteria. Specifically, these students did seem to apply a variety of strategies. Their solution, if accompanied by the list of materials that they discussed, did meet the conditions of the original problem. There was some evidence that they applied strategies they knew (such as guessing and checking or making a list) to this new problem situation. Although this type of problem seemed new to them, they appeared to gain confidence in using their mathematical and problem-solving knowledge, especially through discussing their thinking with each other.

The discussion in the previous paragraph illustrates an important aspect of evaluating problem solving: holistic analysis and assessment are necessary. A general judgment can be made about the mathematical-thinking processes by using a framework that makes sense to one's goals. It is a good idea to use one or two frameworks consistently — perhaps one such as Polya's for specific steps and a more general one for overall development, including attitudes and beliefs. It is also a good idea to develop these frameworks in cooperation with students so that they understand what is important and expected.

Many mathematics teachers and students think that testing must be completely objective, based on correct or incorrect answers. This approach simply does not work in assessing the complex thinking processes that students must develop in problem solving. Students need feedback, monitoring, and evaluation that take into account their individual and creative approaches and recognize the nature of problem solving.

Part Two

PLANNING AND DESIGNING
AN ASSESSMENT PROGRAM

This part of the book deals with the nuts and bolts of planning and developing an alternative assessment program in mathematics. The advice is based on the experience of teachers who over the past two years have worked with students at several grade levels and in a variety of settings. More detailed case descriptions of these experiences are provided in Part Three, where each teacher describes what worked and did not work with their students.

As with any new approach in teaching, alternative assessment takes extra time and work at the beginning. In Chapter Five, some specific hints and ideas are provided for getting started. It makes sense to begin gradually and to make students part of the planning and implementation process. Even young students can provide useful input and will cooperate best if they are involved. Most of all, it is essential to keep in mind that the main purpose of alternative assessment approaches is to improve instruction and learning. New ways of testing and evaluation cannot of themselves have important effects. One of the first considerations in planning new assessments is the kinds of outcomes on which they will be based. If not just tests, what other student products should or could be objects of assessment? Chapter Six outlines a range of student outcomes that can allow for individual differences in learning and productivity, as well as create a closer tie between assessment and instruction. Many of the student products to be evaluated look very much like problems or activities that the teacher may already be using in class. The teacher may even be assigning student grades to these outcomes. The idea here is to make it clear to both teacher and students that these are not only legitimate evaluations of students' mathematics achievement but also that they may be more valid and useful than the traditional tests and quizzes being used.

Techniques for assessing individuals as well as groups are discussed in Chapters Seven and Eight. Current approaches to teaching mathematics include diverse learning settings, ranging from individual to small-group to whole-class activities. Our strategies for assessing students' learning must be aligned with these inst: ictional settings. If students are taught in several modes but evaluated only individually with a common test, they will decide that the other learning activities are less valuable. If we want students to learn how to work and solve problems cooperatively, we must ass ss both the mathematics that they earn in this way and their ability to work together.

Much of what students learn in mathematics depends as much on their attitudes and beliefs about the subject as on their skills and unders anding. In Chapter Nine, we explore ways to assess and monitor student.' beliefs and feelings as they learn and do mathematics. Attitudes go beyond simply liking or disliking mathematics, although that is important. Early in their schooling, students generally develop an idea about what mathematics is all about. Too often, they come to think that all mathematics problems have one answer and there is one way to get that answer. Interest in solving problems, development of a mathematical point of view, and the desire to find reasonableness and patterns in mathematics are important attitudes that should be a part of an assessment plan. Most teachers do not evaluate student attitudes formally. Alternative assessment offers a way to monitor attitudes and beliefs in an integrative fashion as part of an overall evaluation plan.

Chapter Ten addresses how to assign grades, which is one of the first things that concerns teachers when they consider alternative assessment. We have become accustomed to "objective" grading that tends to remove teacher judgment and student self-evaluation from the process. This is exactly the opposite of what we should be doing. Students can learn mathematics best when they are closely involved with teachers in the process of making judgments about their own learning and in taking responsibility for the achievement outcomes. Rather than blaming a test for poor learning or achievement, this approach helps the teacher and students to work together, first to define the criteria for success, then to cooperate in achieving it.

5

GETTING STARTED
IN ALTERNATIVE ASSESSMENT

WHEN TEACHERS ARE ASKED, "WHAT DO YOU VALUE THE MOST, AND WHAT DO you think is most important about mathematics?" most of them say something like, "Being able to solve problems, being able to think, being able to use your mind, being able to actually apply and use ideas in mathematics." But when we look at test scores and what is going on in mathematics classrooms, it appears that many students are not learning the things most teachers value. Instead, most students are learning fairly basic, low-level skills and have difficulty applying even those. If teachers find and develop strategies to assess problem solving and conceptual understanding, they can change the way they teach and the mathematics the students learn.

There are many reasons why students do not achieve as well as they should. One central reason is that we are not measuring what kids really know and can do in mathematics. We only touch the tip of the iceberg with standardized tests. There is evidence that students know more mathematics than even they themselves think. When students are interviewed one on one or are given a chance to demonstrate something involving mathematics, they often surprise people with what they can do. Teachers and other educators must join as colleagues in figuring out the best ways to teach and to assess what our kids can do. We must begin by developing comprehensive plans and procedures for a new approach to assessment.

In this chapter, some suggestions are given for getting started in planning and implementing alternative assessment in a math class. These suggestions have been drawn from experience with a number of teachers, from grade school to high school. Although there are differences from one grade and one school to the next, these are workable ideas. Perhaps the most important advice is to start at the beginning of a school year, to involve the students in planning as much as possible, to be flexible and ready to adapt or revise if an approach does not work, and to be persistent. New assessment takes time and for many students can be unsettling. But the rewards in

35

seeing students learn to understand what they are doing and begin to become confident in their mathematical abilities make the effort worthwhile.

Begin by Choosing a Class

Planning and implementing alternative assessment are complex tasks. The best way to begin is to choose a class and try some things. Teachers have used various criteria that will help them select a class. What group would give the most information? Perhaps one class has the diversity of backgrounds, interests, and abilities that would supply a great deal of information about what works with different types of students. A second approach is to think of the class or group that is the most challenging. This class or group may not be doing well or responding to traditional teaching and assessment and might benefit from a different approach. At the other end of the spectrum, there may be a class that is easy to work with and open to new ideas and approaches. This group would provide the chance to take some risks and be more innovative in trying new kinds of assessment. Finally, a teacher can choose a "typical" class with no special characteristics, needs, or challenges. The assessment alternatives that work with this class should also be effective in similar classes.

Thinking About Outcomes

There are many reasons for changing the way we assess students. Whatever the reasons, the goal is to help students learn mathematics and develop positive attitudes. These outcomes are closely tied to what goes on in mathematics classes. Tests have a great impact on the activities that take place in math classes. The effect is usually to restrict the activities in order to cover the material and get ready for the test. The fastest, most efficient way to cover material is to give a short lecture, do a few examples, then have the students practice similar exercises. But if we want students to learn to solve problems, to reason, to apply their knowledge, and to communicate what they know about mathematics, other activities must be used. As we plan and begin to implement new approaches to assessment, we should think about how often students work at a computer, collaborate on math problems with classmates, do math experiments, use manipulatives, or have class discussions about math problems. And how often do they do exercises in their textbooks, watch the teacher work problems on the board, or do worksheets alone at their desks? Which of these types of activities are most likely to develop problem-solving, reasoning, and communication abilities?

The kinds of activities that teachers use in mathematics have a strong effect on students' attitudes. As already noted, most people experience fear and anxiety toward mathematics. If this attitude is to be changed, we need to think about how students view mathematics. Do they think that learning math is mostly memorizing, that it consists mainly of rules and formulas, and that there is always one correct answer? Or do they believe that math is interesting and fun, that new discoveries are made in math, and that it is OK to estimate and guess when solving math problems? Would they like to take more math courses or consider studying to be a mathematician, an engineer, or a scientist? After all of the courses and tests, these and other attitudes and beliefs are the main things that students take away from their work in math. Recently, one of my students who is preparing to be a mathematics teacher did a little survey, asking her friends and colleagues about their most memorable math teacher. She was horrified to find that each person questioned mentioned something negative. They remembered a teacher's personal habits or their feelings of boredom or even hatred. We know that many of the things we try to do in mathematics result in these kinds of attitudes and recollections. How can new approaches to testing and assessment develop more positive attitudes and at the same time develop better learning?

New Assessment Tasks

As we begin rethinking assessment and testing, the first major point of departure is the type of tasks, questions, or items that will be used to measure mathematical understanding, knowledge, or process. We have already looked at several kinds of assessment tasks, and a great deal more about these will be discussed later in the book. But in order to have something specific to look at, consider the following example:

What two numbers greater than 10 have a product of 736?

This task illustrates several characteristics that an assessment item should have. It encourages and reveals mathematical thinking in a much broader and deeper way than a more traditional item; the teacher then has a chance to observe and evaluate a wide range of student reasoning, mathematical knowledge, and ability to make connections. Students working on this item are likely to see it as a problem to solve. They are likely to assume that different approaches could be used, such as guessing or estimating. If they recognize that the question involves factoring, they can apply their knowledge to obtain several solutions. Some students may use general ideas about factors and products and reason that the two numbers must be even since 736 is even. Finally, students may realize that the numbers could be real numbers, not necessarily whole numbers, leading to a very general statement about the solution. All of these approaches and others provide an opportunity to measure the kind of mathematical knowledge and thinking that we believe is important.

    A more traditional test question such as "find the factors of 736" limits thinking and creates different perceptions about mathematics. This type of question suggests that there is a method or rule for factoring. It implies that factoring is the only approach possible and that there is probably one correct answer. Whether the student gets the answer or not, the teacher receives limited information about how he or she reasons mathematically or connects related mathematical ideas.

New assessment items are likely to be richer, broader tasks. Rather than giving a test with fifty questions, each aimed at a narrow, specific mathematical fact, skill, or concept, teachers should try a test with five items containing many related concepts that require reasoning, problem-solving strategies, and the application of relevant facts and skills. New assessment items or tasks should have three basic criteria:

- A task should give all students the chance to demonstrate some knowledge, skill, and understanding. Students who do not remember how to factor can do something. They can show some skill in multiplying two numbers. A student may come up with 2 and 368, indicating some understanding about factors.
- A task should be rich enough to challenge students to reason and think, to go beyond what they expect they can do and perhaps more than the teacher expects. Students who may never have thought about factor properties may notice that since 36 has a factor of 4, so does 736. Exploration and mathematical reasoning help students to learn new concepts.
- A task should allow the application of a wide range of solution approaches and strategies. One student may try dividing by two or four or six to find a pattern. Another may estimate that the two numbers would be in the twenties and thirties because twenty times thirty is six hundred. Each strategy works and leads to a solution. Students learn that mathematics rewards those who think, reason, and persist in trying different strategies.

Many teachers are concerned about the time and work needed to develop new assessment tasks that have these characteristics. Although it is true that finding and using new tasks can take some time, there are some fairly simple approaches. First, many nonroutine problems that are found in problem collections, and even in textbooks, can be used for assessment. Computational items are easy to adapt. Instead of asking, "find the answer to $.75 \times 5$," there are several alternative questions:

- Why is $.75 \times 5 = 3.75$?
- Make up another problem with the same answer as $.75 \times 5$.
- How much larger is $.76 \times 5$ than $.75 \times 5$?
- Draw a picture to illustrate $.75 \times 5$.

There are many other variations, all of which meet the criteria for alternative assessment tasks. Finally, traditional textbook word problems are a source for constructing good tasks. Alternatives include

- Leave the question off. Ask students to supply it and then solve the problem.
- Make up a problem with the same data and solution but having a different context.
- Provide the answer, and ask students to make up a word problem.

Most teachers find that once they get started on alternative assessment, they begin to notice and think of good tasks. Furthermore, as instruction and evaluation are more closely connected (as discussed in the next section), the need to develop separate assessment tasks diminishes and shifts to finding good problems and situations for teaching mathematical thinking, reasoning, and problem solving.

The Connection Between Assessment and Instruction

Good assessment is an integral part of good teaching. Assessment should not always be seen by students as separated from instruction. Many of the difficulties related to poor attitudes, anxiety, and low achievement begin when the teacher says, "It's time to take a test. Put your books and papers away." Even students who may have performed well during the learning activities and who may have enjoyed discovering new mathematical ideas may not perform up to expectations. Tests often put students into an environment in which time is restricted, resources such as manipulatives and references are not available, and tasks are narrow and possibly meaningless. None of these things have much to do with mathematics, but they do seem to take on more than necessary importance in the classroom evaluation of mathematics learning.

But how can we connect teaching and assessment meaningfully? Part of the answer has to do with our obsession with teaching, testing, and grading each and every detailed piece of information in the curriculum. Change in assessment must be accompanied by change in teaching. The current scenario is to show and tell students how to do a specific skill, then assign twenty or thirty exercises to be corrected and graded. After a week or two, a test is given over each of the five to ten skills that have been "covered." This approach requires a great deal of testing and grading, necessitating quick and easy assessment approaches such as a focus only on the answer, use of multiple-choice tests, and limits on time for tests.

An alternative scenario is to pose a problem or investigation. A day or several days can be spent exploring solutions, trying variations on the problem, and having groups of students present their work, write their solutions, express their thoughts about what they have learned, and discuss how the problem relates to various mathematical concepts. As all of this is going on, students record their work and place it in a folder, and the teacher keeps a checklist of specific mathematical skills and reasoning processes observed during the work. At the end, the teacher assigns grades to the folders, based on a multiple set of criteria that were identified and shared with the students earlier.

In the latter scenario, there are no artificial barriers between teaching, learning, and testing. Students are assessed by looking at what they have produced and how they did it. Pressure to finish, anxiety about taking a test, and reliance on a single type of measure of performance are reduced significantly. The total amount of time taken by the teacher on grading student work is not affected but the way that time is spent is changed a great deal. That time also yields benefits in learning more about how students learn and solve problems. Rather than being forced to look only at answers, the teacher can see processes and the use of strategies and tools for problem solving.

Research studies indicate that higher-order thinking is likely to occur in classrooms that have some identifiable characteristics (Peterson, 1988). These characteristics can be classified into three areas. First, the teacher provides learning activities and an environment in which there is an emphasis on meaning and understanding. Second, there is a classroom atmosphere that encourages student autonomy, persistence, and independent thinking. And third, there is direct teaching of specific problem-solving and reasoning strategies. If assessment is to be aligned with good instruction, it should reflect these characteristics. Evaluation and grades should reward students who are persistent and who use problem-solving strategies. Assessment approaches should focus on the "why," not just the "how," of procedures. Evaluation closely integrated with this type of instruction can communicate strongly what is valued and important in mathematics.

6

STUDENT
MATHEMATICAL PRODUCTS

AN IMPORTANT EMPHASIS OF ALTERNATIVE ASSESSMENT IS ON THE NATURE OF student mathematical products used to judge progress, adapt instruction, make reports to parents, and evaluate the success of the overall mathematics program. Scores on multiple-choice tests, or even partial-credit approaches to more open-ended questions, do not provide sufficiently rich data. A variety of student outcomes and products is necessary in order to assess higher-order thinking skills, integrate assessment with instruction, and develop insights about students' mathematical knowledge. The components of higher-order thinking include problem identification and solution testing, as well as metacognitive skills, such as planning and self-checking. Measures of higher-order thinking include intellectual tasks that call for more than simple information retrieval (Baker, 1990).

We will discuss open-ended questions, performance tasks, investigations, experiments, journals, and portfolios. These are called "power items"; they assess important educational outcomes developed over a period of instructional sequences, emphasize understanding, integrate a number of ideas, and serve as exemplars of good instructional practices (Pandey, 1990). These types of student products are examples of the many different materials on which alternative assessment can be based. They are intended to provide a range of ideas that focus on actual performance and that come closer to what some have termed "authentic" indicators of what students can do — that is, these outcomes are more like the real tasks students may actually do in everyday activities or are more aligned with important mathematical thinking they will need to do in later courses.

Open-Ended Questions

Our discussion will begin with open-ended questions. Many mathematics teachers have used open-ended questions as a regular part of classroom quizzes or tests. However, these questions are not typically used in large-scale assessment. Furthermore, the pressure of large-scale assessment has influenced teachers in greater use of multiple-choice formats in classroom tests. The California Mathematics Council (CMC) has been a leader in stressing the use of open-ended questions as a technique of alternative assessment.

Stenmark (1989) defines an open-ended question as one in which the student is given a situation and is asked to communicate a response, usually in writing. The question may simply ask a student to show the work done on a problem. At the other extreme, an open-ended question can involve complex situations that may require formulating hypotheses, explaining mathematical situations, writing directions, creating new related problems, or making generalizations. These items help match assessment to good classroom questioning strategies. The following is an example of this type of open-ended question:

> A friend says he is thinking of a number. When 100 is divided
> by the number, the answer is between 1 and 2. Give at least
> three statements that must be true of the number. Explain your
> reasoning [Stenmark, 1989, p. 16].

Open-ended questions provide insights into the misconceptions of students and allow the teacher to evaluate the various techniques they use. Further benefits include determining if students can clarify their own thinking, make generalizations, recognize key points in the problem, and organize and interpret information. An open-ended question permits students to display their results using charts, diagrams, or writing for a specific audience. This type of assessment item can also determine if appropriate mathematical language and representation are used by the students.

Other types of open-ended questions provide a chance for students to engage in applications of their knowledge within a more familiar context. Look at the example of an open-ended task found in Figure 6.1, along with the student's response.

In solving the problem, the student has used common sense, along with knowledge about area and perimeter, to propose a reasonable solution to the problem. The student obviously knows and can apply the usual formula for finding the perimeter $[P = 2(l + w)]$ but realizes that the problem calls for a variation on the perimeter in which twice the width plus the length gives the correct answer. The NCTM *Standards* states that the assessment of procedural knowledge should include whether students can recognize the correct procedures and invent or adapt them to fit situations. This task can clearly be used to measure that type of ability.

Effective open-ended tasks go beyond asking students to show their work. Students should be given the chance to explore, to use multiple approaches, and to combine conceptual and procedural knowledge in a setting that has meaning.

Figure 6.1. Concert Stage.

Vanilla Ice has hired you to design the stage for the next concert. The stage should be rectangular and have an area of 1,000 square feet. It will have a security rope on both sides and the front. Make some drawings of different rectangles that have 1,000 square feet of area. How many feet of security rope is needed for each one? Which shape would you use? Why?

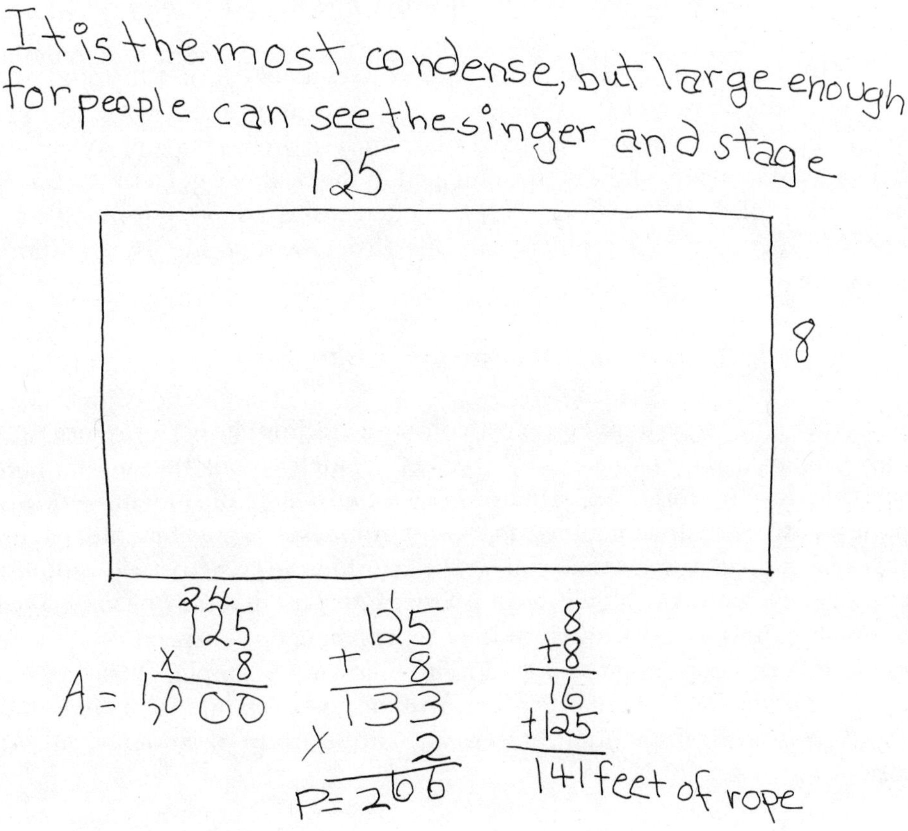

It is the most condense, but large enough for people can see the singer and stage

125

$$A = 1,000$$

$$\begin{array}{r} \overset{2\,4}{1}25 \\ \times\quad 8 \\ \hline 1,000 \end{array}$$

$$\begin{array}{r} 15 \\ +125 \\ \quad 8 \\ \hline 133 \end{array}$$

$$\begin{array}{r} 133 \\ \times\quad 2 \\ \hline P = 266 \end{array}$$

$$\begin{array}{r} 8 \\ +8 \\ \hline 16 \\ +125 \\ \hline 141 \end{array}$$ feet of rope

Teachers are often concerned about the time and effort necessary to develop good open-ended tasks. Problem books, challenge questions from textbooks, and supplementary mathematics materials are all good sources. A simple and readily available source is the standard word problems found in textbooks. As they are written, most word problems are fairly closed and uninteresting exercises. They usually expect students to apply and practice a recently learned algorithm. But with fairly simple adaptations, textbook word problems can provide ideas for open-ended assessment tasks. Consider the following example:

Original version: Two children wish to buy a present for their parents that costs $50. If one of them has saved $15, how much more money do they need?

Modified version: Use a catalog or advertising section from the newspaper to pick out a gift for your mother or father that costs between $10 and $15. Make up a plan to show how you could earn and save enough money for the present. Include in your plan how much you could earn and how long it would take.

In the modified version, the task is personalized, and the student is placed at the center of the problem. Another way to modify the problem would be to let the student make a plan for a fictitious person. When students become a part of the story, engaged in the task, we get a much clearer assessment of their knowledge. Open-ended tasks, adapted to involve students in solving a real problem, are the easiest way to modify traditional assessment.

Performance Tasks

In mathematics, perhaps the most common traditional performance tasks have involved physical activities such as geometric constructions or measuring. More recently, performances are a component of student work with manipulatives such as geoboards, base-ten blocks, or algebra tiles. These types of performances are an integral part of learning activities leading to concept development. However, it is also important that they become a part of mathematics assessment since they represent central aspects of students' mathematical knowledge and skill. The following examples illustrate how manipulatives might be used in performance assessment. Items like these could be used in individual interviews, with a group of students, or with an entire class.

a. Use the geoboard and the red rubber band to make a right triangle whose legs are 1 unit and 3 units long. Draw the triangle you have made on the dot paper. Explain why the area of the triangle is 1 ½ square units.

b. Use the algebra tiles to show why $2x + 5x - 3x = 4x$.

c. Here is a rectangle. About how many centimeters long would you estimate its perimeter to be? Use the ruler to measure the perimeter. How close was your estimate?

It is important that assessment and instruction be closely aligned. Teachers often use manipulatives to teach but move too quickly to symbolic and other abstract representations in order to get their students ready for a test. Sometimes, we assume that students do not really know a concept or procedure unless they can demonstrate or calculate using traditional mathematical symbolism. In fact, research has shown that many students who have mastered the symbolic manipulations have a very fragile understanding of the concepts. For example, many ninth- or tenth-grade students could correctly choose the picture of a right triangle and its area on multiple-choice items. Fewer of them would be able to perform a task such as contained in Item a. Performance assessment requires generating a product drawn from an understanding of concepts and the ability to synthesize relationships. These are higher-order thinking abilities that go beyond choosing among alternatives. Items b and c require similar higher-order thinking. And although it would be possible to assess students' understanding of the relationship described in Item b, it is difficult to see how skills such as estimation and measurement can be assessed completely without some type of actual hands-on performance.

Modern assessment practice intends to go beyond the traditional performances in order to extend and enrich students' knowledge. New technology, especially calculators and computers, create great opportunities for student performances, both in operating the technology itself and in applying it in learning activities or problem-solving situations. The following items offer examples:

d. Use a spreadsheet program to make a table of multiples of the first five whole numbers.

e. Write a LOGO program that draws a square inside of a square so that the vertices of the inside square are at the midpoints of the sides of the outside square.

f. Use the TI-81 calculator to draw the graph of $y = 2\sin3x$. Set the ranges for x and y so that two full periods of the graph appear on the screen. Use the Trace key to find the coordinates where the graph crosses the x-axis.

Each of these performance tasks requires the student to have knowledge of how to use the technology. Item f focuses directly on the use of the calculator. Item d is more general; it is aimed at determining the student's knowledge and skill in using a piece of software to solve a problem. In Item e, the software is a tool helping to carry out a task.

Performance tasks have two major dimensions: the recording of behavior, such as conducting an experiment, and the rating of the resulting products (Baker, 1990). These tasks may be assigned to groups or individuals and may take more than one class period to complete. A good task has the goal of arousing the students' curiosity. Other technological tools can be incorporated into a performance assessment problem, such as videotaping the task while the students are completing it or having the students make a video- or audiotape. As part of the assessment, students may evaluate other students for part of the score. With the use of performance assessment items, other content areas can be integrated with a math assignment to enhance the task or broaden the students' abilities.

Similar to open-ended questions, performance assessment items have several advantages. Teachers are able to examine students' abilities to work together in groups or individually. Flexibility in thinking and problem solving through a variety of modes can be examined. It is, of course, also possible to assess the skill and use of manipulatives, equipment, calculators, or computers directly. Furthermore, we can measure students' use of a scientific method, such as the ability to formulate hypotheses, design an experiment and investigations, and test hypotheses. Performances should be a central focus of alternative assessment because they are at the heart of learning mathematics through hands-on activity.

Investigations and Experiments

Investigations and experiments are examples of other important types of hands-on activities that can be used for assessment. These incorporate various tools for learning mathematics and provide the opportunity for long-term or self-directed work. Many of our objectives for problem solving and interdisciplinary content can be achieved through student investigations, done either by individuals, teams, or groups. The experiments may be science-oriented, using mathematical skills (for instance, studying the behavior of a pendulum), or mathematically based (like explorations with procedures or patterns). The following items are examples of these types of assessment tasks.

> g. You are an expert dietician. You have taken on the job of planning one week's menu of three balanced meals per day for a family of four: two adults, a six-year-old boy, and a thirteen-year-old girl. Consult the latest recommendations of the National Academy of Science and other sources for nutritional requirements for adults and children. Write your menu for the week. Using grocery ads from newspapers, determine the cost per week for your recommended menu.
>
> h. You are a famous designer. Sketch several outfits for men or women. For two of the outfits, make a list of the materials needed to make them. Figure out how much each outfit would cost to make, including materials and labor. Compare prices of outfits similar to your designs in catalogs.
>
> i. The Earthquake Information Center provides the location and other data for earthquakes throughout the world. Use a computer modem to gain access to this information, and keep track

of earthquake data for a month. Record the locations on a world map. Find a way to record the strength and other data for each earthquake. Write a report of your findings, including any patterns in location or frequency of earthquakes.

Using investigations and experiments as assessment items gives a view of the students' ability to hypothesize, analyze, and synthesize data. These tasks also allow students to think in many modes, use creativity and ingenuity, and persist in a long-term project. In other words, experiments and investigations help us evaluate higher-order thinking skills.

Many teachers avoid student investigations because they take time and are difficult to assess, especially if students work in groups. Many of these concerns are addressed in Chapters Eight and Ten. The goals set out by the NCTM *Standards* stress the importance of students' making connections among mathematical topics and in linking mathematics with the sciences and other subject areas. Projects and investigations are an ideal approach to meeting these goals. Although careful planning is needed, a project can also address more traditional mathematics content objectives as well. Many projects involve doing calculations, preparing graphs, making measurements, and demonstrating other important procedures and skills. Instruction on these and related skills can take place within the context of a long-term project. Assessment can take place in an ongoing fashion, as well as at the conclusion of the experiment or investigation.

As with the other types of student products, experiments and investigations offer an alternative and enriched environment to gauge students' mathematical learning, especially in higher-order thinking. The difficulty in assigning scores or grades need not be a deterrent to using these helpful teaching strategies.

Student Journals

Many teachers have their students keep a notebook containing class notes. Notes are important resources for outside study, such as examples from class, and for information to review before tests. In alternative assessment approaches, the journal goes beyond note taking. A journal can be used to evaluate not only knowledge but the ways students think. The journal can be an outlet and a communications link; it permits students to write about their feelings, attitudes, and areas of difficulty or enjoyment in the mathematics they are studying. Moreover, a journal can become an avenue for self-reporting wherein students assess their own abilities or reflect on their problem-solving strategies. Journals can be used to monitor metacognitive development by having students write about mathematical concepts they understand or do not understand and skills they can or cannot perform.

Mathematical communication skills and abilities are one of the areas emphasized by the NCTM *Standards*. Perhaps the most important way to achieve this standard is to create the opportunity for students to write mathematically. At first, many find this type of writing very difficult. At the beginning, they may be asked to write how they solved a problem or to keep a record of daily problem-solving activities. Some teachers have found success in asking students to pretend they are writing a letter about math class to a friend, or to write simple explanations of how to do a problem for a student at a lower grade level. Other teachers have provided an outline or a set of questions for students to follow in writing about a problem or about what they have learned. The example shown in Exhibit 6.1 might be an outline to help students spend five to ten minutes reflecting and writing about what they learned in class.

Exhibit 6.1. Sample Journal Outline.

Journal entry # _____   Name _____
Date _____

Today's math topic:

Two important ideas:

What I understood best:

What I need more work on:

How this topic can be used in real life:

Journals can be used to gather information concerning noncognitive aspects, such as the students' interests, their persistence, and changes in their attitudes toward mathematics; students answer reflective questions like "What do you like best about _____ ?" "How have you thought about the problem?" "What did you discover?" Through journal writing, students are given a private place to address concerns they would not otherwise express or reveal to the teacher.

Assigning grades to journals must be approached with care and sensitivity. If the journal is aimed at having students tell about their attitudes or feelings, it may be a good idea to assign a completion grade, rather than a point or letter grade. Even in the case of written descriptions of problem-solving processes, it is important not to discourage creativity. The primary purpose of journals is to foster communication. Practice and positive reinforcement are better than trying for perfection right away.

Portfolios of Student Products

More than any other aspect of alternative assessment, the idea of a portfolio seems to have gained the most attention. The concept of a portfolio comes from performing professions such as art, photography, and architecture, where people include samples of their best works in a range of settings. The value of collecting students' work in a mathematical portfolio is gaining wide acceptance. Currently, the Vermont Department of Education (1990) is using portfolios for state mathematics assessment. Much of what we will discuss is based on Vermont's experience.

A portfolio should be designed to illustrate the various talents of students, some of whom by traditional testing are considered to lack mathematical ability. For some students, the anxiety of taking a formal test can limit their performance. Others are more reflective and need extended time to think through problems. Others do their best mathematical thinking through hands-on performance or work on projects and activities. For still others, an opportunity to write or to explain concepts orally can open the way to better performance. These and other individual differences in how students display their mathematical knowledge are the strongest arguments for multiple assessments. A portfolio provides a structure not only for collecting and validating these, but also for including them as legitimate bases for evaluation. Through the use of portfolios, all students are able to demonstrate their talents and to learn essential ideas about what is important in mathematics and why.

Portfolios have the great advantage of creating at the same time a diagnostic, formative, and summative record. They furnish the crucial information about students' weaknesses and strengths that teachers need in order to adjust instruction. Portfolios recognize different learning styles, making assessment less culture-dependent and less biased (Stenmark, 1989). Portfolios also provide the kind of rich and comprehensive picture of student abilities that is essential in making decisions such as placement into advanced classes or career counseling.

An early and major decision about a portfolio has to do with its purpose and use. The teacher, student, parent, and administrator may have different but complementary purposes. For example, a teacher may be interested in measuring a student's mathematical development or in providing the opportunity to demonstrate mathematical knowledge in alternative ways; the portfolio, from the teacher's perspective, offers a broad, valid basis for student assessment and evaluation. A student may want only the very best work kept in the portfolio, reflecting only areas of strength and resulting in the best overall grade. A parent may want the portfolio as a record or "keepsake" of everything the child has done. And administrators may wish to have student portfolios simply to illustrate that their school is at the leading edge of assessment practice. As the portfolio is planned, decisions about the purpose of the portfolio should be clear to everyone and should probably be put in writing, along with a list of both criteria for placing items in the portfolio and categories of materials to be included.

Portfolios can represent diverse tasks, allowing achievement to be shown in a variety of ways and supplying an overall picture of mathematical knowledge. Offering concrete examples of students' work as a basis for eliciting support and establishing clear standards, portfolios can be an essential tool for conferences with parents. An innovative use of portfolios can be with administrators who evaluate teaching. Rather than relying on a single lesson or a class test average to judge overall teaching effectiveness, an administrator can turn to student portfolios for rich evidence of mathematical learning outcomes.

The selection of items to include in a portfolio is closely related to its purpose and is a key decision that can involve the student, teacher, and parents. Many teachers and schools have developed comprehensive procedures for working with parents and students to implement portfolios. Teachers consult with the students and communicate with the parents to aid them in deciding what pieces to contribute. Ideally, the students should have an opportunity to include what they think is best, since this approach aids in the development of the metacognitive ability of self-checking. Parents' involvement can help to communicate the focus of the mathematics program and the importance of their support in enhancing students' development of mathematical skills and confidence.

Portfolios should be designed to focus on conceptual understanding, problem solving, reasoning, and communication abilities. Portfolios should not simply be files in which to collect drill and practice exercises and work on other discrete skills, nor should they simply be a repository of everything the student has done. Many of the student products previously discussed in this chapter, along with others, are examples of what is appropriate. Evidence of these key abilities may include photos of projects, students' descriptions and reports of projects, and audio- or videotapes of performances.

The number of items to include in a portfolio is highly variable, but too many cloud the picture. Ten or twelve pieces are considered adequate. Some teachers feel that items should be included at various times, such as at the beginning, middle, and end of a grading period or year, with the option of updating particular items. The collected tasks may be student-writing pieces dealing with mathematical topics. Sample items may be from group or individual projects the students have created.

The involvement of the student in selecting, structuring, reviewing, and reflecting on the portfolio is as important as the actual contents. Many teachers include these processes as a part of the structure and requirements for the portfolio. Students develop an organizational structure and table of contents for the portfolio, which includes a title, brief description of each item, and other pertinent information: dates, mathematical content, and names of other students who might have participated in the portfolio's development. Students are often asked to provide a rationale for choosing each item, whether it was a chance to learn a difficult concept, a task they especially enjoyed doing, or a problem they thought was significant. Finally, students are sometimes asked to write a summary of the important mathematical concepts and strategies they have learned. This task serves as a synthesis for a major unit or time period of work. Mathematics is frequently seen by students as a set of discrete and unrelated ideas, rules, and procedures. The portfolio provides a context for helping students see a larger picture, for synthesizing their learning, and reflecting on important ideas. This approach serves to empower students; it gives them a sense of control and responsibility for their own mathematical learning.

7

INDIVIDUAL
MATHEMATICAL PERFORMANCE

TRADITIONALLY, MATHEMATICS TEACHERS HAVE EMPLOYED PAPER-AND-PENCIL quizzes and tests, completed by an individual student without discussion and without other tools within a fixed time period. These tests were the sole measure of the mastery of mathematics objectives. Although many teachers construct their own, reliance on tests prepared by textbook publishers has become more and more prevalent in recent years. These textbook tests are far removed from the specific conditions and needs of a particular class or student.

There are some variations on this pattern, including the use of homework and in-class assignments as components of individual evaluation. This approach to mathematics assessment seems quite logical and is accepted as appropriate by most teachers and students. It is only when we consider the wide range of individual variations in ability, modes of thinking, and interests that we pause to wonder if traditional approaches really are valid for most students. Furthermore, when we take into account the many types of mathematical knowledge, skills, performances, and thinking processes, we wonder how all of these can possibly be evaluated with a single approach.

Mathematics has changed. Computation has become a minor goal, giving way to estimation, problem solving, use of computers, representation with manipulatives and spreadsheets, and many other performance-related outcomes. Group-administered paper-and-pencil tests, which are appropriate for measuring computational skills, just do not work in assessing these other outcomes. Group assessment and paper-and-pencil tests have gradually impoverished efforts to teach and assess a great deal of important mathematics. In order to teach and evaluate performance-related mathematics, individual work must be the focus.

Focus on the Individual

Recently, I persuaded some middle school teachers to assess their students' problem-solving processes with a few nonroutine, open-ended tasks. We worked together to develop some tasks that corresponded to a unit on area and perimeter they were finishing near the end of the school year. Some teachers tried the tasks with students working in groups; others asked students to do them individually. Here is an example of one of the tasks.

Kathy's Dog Pen

Kathy is building a pen for her dog. She has 64 feet of fencing and wants to build it in the shape of a rectangle. Make some drawings of rectangles that Kathy could make that would use all 64 feet of the fence. Which one of these rectangles do you think she should build? Why?

An immediate reaction from most teachers upon seeing responses to this task is to ask questions about what the students did or might have been thinking about. When several papers from students are seen, it is striking and obvious to see the individual differences among them. Although it may be easy to ignore individual differences and performances when looking at multiple-choice or short-answer tests, it is impossible to overlook them in a task like this.

A great deal can be learned, even from papers such as the one by the student who says "I give up" (Figure 7.1). For example, this student did draw a very good rectangle before giving up. The student also understands the concept of reflection. It would be interesting to ask this person in an individual setting to draw a reflection of a rectangle or to find a rectangle that could be reflected in its diagonal.

The second student (Figure 7.2) has the idea that the best figure would be a square, having chosen the rectangle that is the "squarest." This student may hold the very common misconception that a square is not a rectangle. Of course, there are other rectangles, such as one that is fifteen by seventeen feet, that are even closer to being squares, but this student seems to be limited to even numbers as sides. Many of the students did the same thing. Why do odd-numbered sides seem less appropriate? This is another of the many questions that would be terrific to explore with individual students.

The other two students (Figures 7.3 and 7.4) identified the square as having the greatest area. The last student (Figure 7.4) clearly has well-connected knowledge of the concepts of square and rectangle and did not bother to draw other examples. The student either knew the relationship before or reasoned that sixty-four divided by four is sixteen in the process of solving the problem. By the way, some teachers insisted that this student not be given full credit because directions were not followed to draw several rectangles.

Overall, the results were complex and different for everyone. The one common reaction by the teachers was that they discovered that some students had previously unknown skills, knowledge, and ways of thinking. They

Figure 7.1. First Sample Response to Dog-Pen Task.

Figure 7.2. Second Sample Response to Dog-Pen Task.

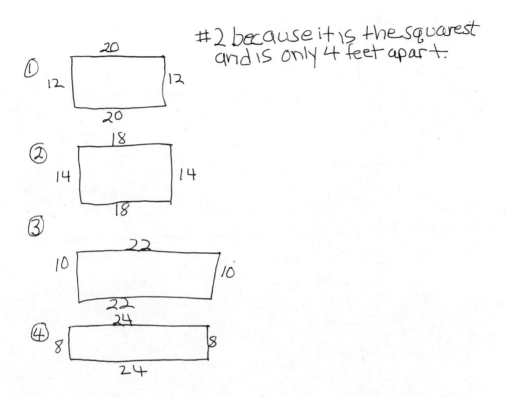

#2 because it is the squarest and is only 4 feet apart.

also noticed that some students whom they had thought were very capable did miserably. Every teacher said they wished they had done this before and vowed to do more assessment this way in the coming school year. These were excellent, conscientious teachers who thought they knew their students' mathematical knowledge very well. But the traditional assessments they were using missed a great deal.

The purpose of most testing, whether it is a teacher-made quiz, a publisher-developed chapter test, or a commercial standardized test, is to compare the student to some predetermined or standard norm. Students are placed along a continuum based on external criteria without regard to their differences or special abilities. Although some of these types of tests may be necessary to determine achievement in basic skills for large populations, their usefulness in classrooms and for individual students is very limited. In the 1980s, more and more teachers and school districts felt forced to teach with an eye to such tests. Ironically, the more this practice continued, the less focus there was on individual students. Like those in my experiment, teachers had nearly lost touch with the capabilities their students actually had or did not have. The time required to cover material and to practice for standardized, external tests reduced teachers' ability to do real, common-sense, individual assessment.

Figure 7.3. Third Sample Response to Dog-Pen Task.

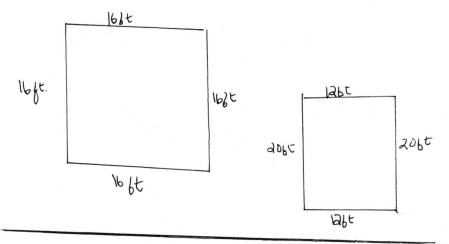

She should use the square pen because it has more area and is easier to build

ruler calclator

At the end of the year, teachers are often asked to recommend students for courses for the following year. This decision can affect a student for the rest of his or her life. How does the teacher decide which course to recommend? If the decision is based on the teacher's judgment of the student's overall ability, how is this opinion formed? Should the decision be based on the results of standardized tests? Should the recommendation be based upon grades that usually are the result of chapter tests and homework? Teachers make important decisions about individual students every day. They need strategies that enable them to base these decisions on the very best information.

Being Efficient and Balancing Priorities

In most American schools, teachers interact with 20 to 30, even 40, students at a time. In the upper grades, many teachers see 150 students a day in five or six periods. It is an incredible challenge to motivate and teach this many students every day, let alone know each one's abilities and differences. More than anything, the structure of schools and classes has probably been most responsible for the type of assessment practices used. It is efficient and makes teachers feel they are objective and fair. But even if teachers had smaller classes, would they know how to use better strategies

Figure 7.4. Fourth Sample Response to Dog-Pen Task.

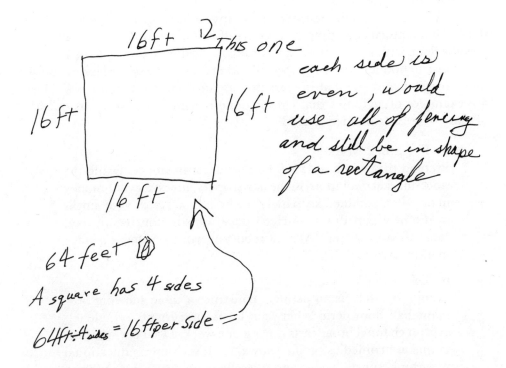

that could measure complex mathematical knowledge and abilities, provide useful feedback to students, and help develop improved teaching methods?

A first essential shift is to broaden the purposes and priorities for assessment. Assigning grades is not the only or most important goal of testing. The real one is to help children develop mathematical power. A second crucial change is to expand the types of strategies used for assessment. Simply using nonroutine, open-ended items from time to time can make a real impact, without increasing the work load significantly. Finally, we must balance the need to prepare students for standardized tests with the need to develop their individual mathematical abilities. Many state assessments and commercial tests are already emphasizing performances and problem solving, so this task may not be as difficult as it has been in the past. In fact, teachers may find that their classroom evaluation approaches will need to change in order to catch up to the expectations of some state assessments.

Expanded Settings for Assessment

Many of the tasks and student performances discussed in Chapter Six offer excellent ways of developing an expanded picture of each student's mathematical power. Journals, projects, and investigations are all settings allowing for personal creativity and varying approaches to a problem or project.

Self-confidence and self-esteem are critical in the development of youngsters, especially in mathematics.

Many mathematics teachers avoid investigations or projects because they take too much class time or are too difficult to control. Yet not all tasks need be done within the classroom. A range of options can supplement traditional instruction and testing, especially where large classes or lack of equipment or space may prevent in-class investigations or hands-on work. Here are examples of activities that can be done by individual students outside of class over an extended period:

a. The Stock Market
Pretend that you have $500,000 to invest in stocks. Using the stock-market quotations in the newspapers, invest all your money in one day, and then keep daily record as you watch your stocks in the newspapers for fourteen days. On the fourteenth day, "sell" all your stocks. Write a report on your results as a stock market investor!

b. Television Watching
Using your television listings, construct a table showing how many half-hour periods between 1 P.M. and 7 P.M. a single television channel broadcasts during one week. Decide which programs are comedies, game shows, serious drama, educational programs, sports, news, and miscellaneous programs. Make a graph to illustrate these facts. Write a report on what you found.

c. "Floating 2"
I am thinking of a number. Its first digit (on the far left) is a 2. When I "float" the 2 from the far left to the far right, I get the same result as if I just triple my original number. Find my number.
Example: Is the number 268? No, since floating the 2 gives us 682, which is not equal to 3 times 268.

These activities do not require special equipment and could be done by most students, regardless of the availability of resources at home. They are clear and direct enough for most students to have some success, but sufficiently open for nearly everyone to apply a certain amount of individual creativity or insight. Depending on the grade level, each of the activities could be expanded to address more abstract or complex mathematical ideas. A general framework such as the ones discussed in Chapters Four and Ten can be used to judge student outcomes, provide feedback, and build a profile of individual problem-solving strengths and areas for further development.

Student Interviews

In a recent project on assessment, one of the fourth-grade teachers decided to try and interview each of her students to determine their problems or interests in mathematics. One boy had been having behavioral problems in class, and the teacher was unhappy with his performance. During the course of the interview, the boy revealed that he really loved math. The teacher was completely surprised to find this out. The boy would never have said it in public, and his other problems tended to hide this special interest. The teacher said that her attitude toward him changed. She began to build on his interest in math, helping him to improve his overall performance. She plans to take time to talk individually with each child as often as she can as long as she teaches.

Individual interviews can be designed to accomplish many objectives in assessment, from determining specific skill development to just finding out about problems and interests or how students are doing. Many teachers feel that individual interviews are impossible to manage, especially when they must teach 150 students or if they must cover six or seven subjects during the day. Yet a great deal can be done, just by greeting students at the door. "How are you?" "Is there anything wrong?" "How did you do on last night's assignment?" This is an example of an informal interview that can take place throughout the day. Notes or other informal checklists can be used to develop long-term records of progress or patterns.

Some teachers overcome the time and number constraints by interviewing three or four students at a time or by spreading out the interviews so that each student is contacted at least once every grading period. Although this solution may seem to be less than ideal, it is much better than the usual case in which many timid students can go through years of school and never spend time talking individually with a teacher. If interviews are conducted regularly, students view them as an integral part of the classroom experience, not always as assessments or evaluations.

One teacher used an innovative approach in order to have individual interviews with each student as part of the semester exam (Kulm & Lockmandy, 1976). In the interviews, which occurred over the course of a week, students chose two or three problems by drawing problem cards from a box and solving them while explaining their reasoning to the teacher. Her colleagues helped by supervising her classes during preparation periods when students not being interviewed reviewed material for the oral exam. She interviewed other students during their study periods. It took a great deal of cooperation and effort, but the teacher believed the oral exam was the only valid approach to assess students' real mathematical abilities. It also encouraged students to prepare so that they understood what they were doing, rather than just know the answer.

Planning and Conducting Interviews

Let's look at the interview more formally as an assessment technique for individuals. Ernest (1992) suggests that the advantages of formal interviews include the students' opportunity to communicate orally and the teacher's flexibility to adapt questions as the need arises. The advantages of oral communication are threefold:

- A student may respond directly or actively to a physical task, making it possible to determine more accurately whether a student has specific skills. For example, a student might be asked to measure the length of a table so the teacher can directly observe her or his performance.
- A younger or second-language student who has difficulty reading can respond verbally to a question allowing assessment of a broader range of thinking.
- A student may find it easier to operate at a high cognitive level — to make judgments, justify, evaluate, and express opinions.

As for the teacher, he or she may prompt, stimulate, or guide the student if needed. Teachers can then give credit to the successful students who do not need help, without failing the ones who can be successful with a little prompting. The second advantage is that the teacher can focus on the strengths, skills, and interests of students. For example, while discussing a project, the student may communicate enthusiasm, likes, and dislikes for the project.

Structured Interviews

There are three steps in developing and conducting a structured interview. First, before the interview takes place, select the assessment objectives. Second, construct a general set of oral questions in a sequence based on the objectives, and prepare a detailed response sheet to record (a) the student's response and (b) what type of help was given. Finally, carry out the interview, and record responses to show unaided success, success with or without aid, and lack of success. A suggested coding scheme is outlined here:

S — successful; the student gives an answer or solution spontaneously and without clear difficulty. The student may hesitate, think, or do calculations but does so with a plan or clear direction in mind. The approach need not be the most efficient or standard one.

P — prompted; the student may require a brief hint or prompt, such as pointing to essential information that may have been overlooked, clarifying a term or word, or posing a question for getting started.

U — unsuccessful; the student gives an incorrect or seriously incomplete answer or explanation. The student may use incorrect terms, formulas, or approaches illustrating incomplete or no understanding.

N — no answer; the student is unable to respond and indicates little or no understanding of the question or problem, even after a hint or prompt.

T — teach; following a very unsuccessful attempt or no answer, the teacher may choose to teach the concept or procedure in order to go on with the interview. A single gap in knowledge can sometimes be overcome in this way, making the rest of the interview a more valid assessment of the student's true knowledge or skill.

Figure 7.5. Interview Guide.

Student name _____   Date _____

Concepts: measures—straight and curved lines
             geometry—rectangle and circle

Apparatus: sheet with rectangle
             sheet with circle
             ruler
             pencil
             scrap paper, string, scissors, tape

Codes: S—successful; spontaneous correct response
             P—prompted; correct response after receiving a hint or prompt
             U—unsuccessful; incorrect or inappropriate answer
             N—no answer; did not respond; did not know
             T—teach; instruction provided before proceeding

1. "What do we mean by the perimeter of a rectangle?"

Student response	Code	Comments

2. Present the sheet with a drawing of a rectangle.

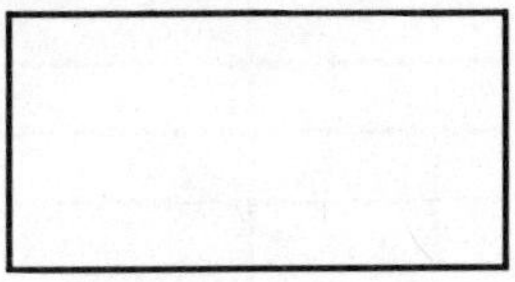

"Could you show me the perimeter of this rectangle?"

Student response	Code	Comments

3. "How would you measure the perimeter of a rectangle?"

Student response	Code	Comments

Figure 7.5. Interview Guide, Cont'd.

4. "Show me how you would estimate the length of the perimeter of this rectangle. What is the estimate?"

Student response	Code	Comments

5. Present a ruler to the student. "Check your estimate by measuring."

Student response	Code	Comments

6. "Is there any other method for finding the perimeter without measuring all four sides? Show me."

Student response	Code	Comments

Source: Adapted from Ernest, 1992, and Assessment of Performance Unit, 1980.

In Figure 7.5, we see a sample of the type of interview guide that can be used during the interview to take notes on a student's responses. The guide is also helpful following the interview, using mental notes or, preferably, a tape recording of the session. The sample is taken from Paul Ernest's *Mathematics Teaching: State of the Art* (1992, pp. 56–71).

This structured interview provides the opportunity to assess specific mathematical knowledge, skills, and concepts. It is a good idea, especially in the first interview you do or where you wish to assess specific knowledge, to use this type of structured interview. Clearly, the codes can be converted into numerical values and combined in various ways to obtain a score or grade. A great advantage of the coding system is that a student need not be failed if he or she reaches an impasse or is unsure of one of the questions. With some prompting or even teaching, the rest of the interview can proceed; the teacher can evaluate what the student knows, rather than focusing only on what is not known.

Obviously, this approach also combines assessment with instruction, turning the evaluation into a teaching opportunity if a student needs help. Of course, if a student is hopelessly lost or confused, the scoring or grading objective can be abandoned, and the interview session can become a tutorial for a student who needs one-on-one attention.

Problem- or Project-Based Interviews

A very useful approach is to base an interview on a completed piece of work. Questions can be directed toward a solution to an open-ended problem, a completed project, a model the student has built, or a report on a mathematical investigation. Questions may ask the student to describe any difficulties in completing the task, to evaluate sections of it, or to suggest ways of improving it. The interview can bring closure to a student's extended math work and permit assessment in an area of his or her choice. Consider again one of the examples of student responses to the open-ended problem illustrated at the beginning of the chapter (Figure 7.2). What are some questions that might be asked in a follow-up interview in which we wish to look more carefully at the student's understanding or possible misconceptions?
Here are some possible questions:

- What do you mean by "squarest"?
- Is a square a rectangle? Why do you say that?
- What is your definition of a rectangle?
- Please draw a rectangle that has odd numbers for the measure of its sides and uses sixty-four feet of fence.
- What is the area of each of your rectangles? Which one has the greatest area?
- What is the relationship between the area and the shape of your rectangles?

A four- or five-level scoring rubric for each question might be developed, ranging from a top score, given for a complete and correct response, to the lowest score, indicating confusion or an incorrect or absent response. Again, if desired, any of the questions could be taken as an opportunity to teach the unknown or incorrect concepts. If a group of students has completed a project or a joint task, then the same process can take place; individual students can be interviewed to assess their understanding of and contribution to the group's work.

Suggestions for Interviewing

According to Stenmark (1989), the questioning sequence, whether in a formal or informal setting, should begin at the student's comfort level. The questions should begin with broad, general questions followed by increasingly specific ones as the teacher tries to determine what makes sense to the student. There should also be an adequate pause after a question, giving the student time to think through a response or reconsider a previous response.

Interviews allow teachers to get to know their students both mathematically and personally, a familiarity that helps to establish a caring classroom environment. Interviews involve planning to establish the proper logistics. A teacher may conduct formal, highly structured interviews or less-structured, informal questioning. Interviews permit students to think at a high cognitive level, often revealing mathematical knowledge and skills beyond teachers' expectations.

8

GROUP
MATHEMATICAL PERFORMANCE

A KEY FINDING IN RECENT RESEARCH ON LEARNING, INCLUDING THAT OF HIGHER-order thinking in mathematics, is the effectiveness of small-group instruction. In addition to the benefits that many students derive from learning in a group setting, business leaders are asking that students learn to work cooperatively on tasks. Since many educators are answering the call by allowing their students to learn together, there is a need to assess this type of activity. One of the first questions that may come to mind is which type of learning is appropriate for group assessment. Some mathematics educators may agree that problem solving is one kind. Other types of appropriate activities might include performance tasks such as measurement, computer work, or investigations and projects. These examples suggest that there are a number of questions to consider in evaluating group work:

- What types of mathematical learning are appropriate for the measurement of group learning? Discovery lessons, extended projects, informal exploration, and problem solving are examples of activities often assessed as a part of group learning.
- Which learning contexts require alternative assessment approaches for evaluating group learning? Group interaction and performance with manipulatives such as measuring devices, computers, and other tools are examples of settings that are less amenable to traditional testing.
- Is there a point in the instructional sequence that is more suited for group assessment? Often, group work is used during practice or review, during laboratory work, or on long-term projects.
- How can the teacher simultaneously monitor and evaluate group performance?
- What type of rating system should be employed? Should the scales focus on mathematical knowledge and performance, group processes and interaction, or both?

65

- Should the teacher assess individuals within the group or the group as a whole?
- How should grades be assigned: individually, to the group, or both?

The basic goal of all these questions is to decide what we are trying to assess. Most teachers' answer is that there are two primary areas of interest, mathematical performance and group processes. While it is obvious that the main priority is for students to learn mathematics, it is also important that they learn to work together. Effective group work not only helps to make students more productive citizens but it also helps them to learn mathematics. The assessment of group processes thus has a basic link to the primary goal of learning mathematics. In the remainder of this chapter, we summarize some practical issues in group instruction, then provide some specific examples and ideas for assessing group learning and interaction in a mathematics classroom.

Practical Issues

It is difficult to separate the questions of group instruction versus group assessment strategies. Although it is beyond the scope of this chapter to examine how group instruction can be used in mathematics, we will address some of the general issues that often arise. Obviously, unless a teacher uses group work during instruction, it is impossible to implement group assessment. The main idea is that assessment and instruction should be integrated as much as possible, and that integration includes instruction in small groups.

There are many practical concerns that face teachers who use small-group instruction. Most of these arise from the students involved and the preferences of the teacher; there are few hard and fast rules. What the size of the groups should be, whether they should be matched on ability, and which students should work together are some of the decisions that must be made. Another set of issues has to do with the management of small-group instruction. These questions involve how often it should be used, the availability and use of hands-on materials, discipline or noise problems, and coverage of material. These kinds of issues may have implications for the assessment of content learning and of group processes. It may be necessary to try variations so that students are not penalized by certain group arrangements.

A real concern of teachers is that group work is unstructured and can lead to disorder. In order to avoid this problem, it is important to start with short activities that are structured; they require that a specific set of steps be carried out and assign clear roles and activities for each member. For example, in a tenth-grade geometry class, a first outdoor activity might be to measure the distance from point A to point B. One student holds the tape measure; a second student holds the end of the tape and uses sticks to mark tape-measure lengths; a third lines up the first two students and makes sure that they follow a straight line; and a fourth records the measurements. Everyone in the group has a specific job, and there is a clear procedure to follow. After doing this type of activity and learning to work together for a month or two, students may be able to take on a group activity assignment such as "Go out and make a map of the schoolyard." Even teachers and students who have worked in groups for some time might consider more structured activities the first few times that assessment is introduced. These will make it possible to identify clearly group roles and the way each component of the students' performance will be evaluated.

Teachers who have not had a great deal of experience with group instruction may be especially concerned about how students will interact. Teachers worry that some students will be lazy and let the most motivated or able members do all the work (about which more later). Or they fear that some students will not want to help each other or will be reluctant to share all of their information. Some students in mainstreamed classes may be emotionally disturbed and have difficulties with social interaction. The best approach for many teachers is to assign specific roles for each member of a group and periodically rotate assignments. Typical group member roles are the leader, who oversees the group's work and acts as a liaison between the group and the teacher; the manager, who keeps track of time and makes sure that each group member understands and participates; the reporter, who records notes and reports all findings to the class, including a presentation or summary if requested; and the organizer, who gathers the necessary materials, is responsible for their proper use, and returns them.

An important element in measuring group performance is to decide prior to the activity what aspects of the group's work will be assessed and to communicate these expectations to the students. When students know that a certain behavior is expected and that their work as a member of a group will be assessed, many of the concerns about group work are alleviated.

Assessing Individual and Group Learning

Perhaps the most controversial part of this assessment is how much emphasis or weight is placed on the work of the group. Problems generally have to do with inequities in the contribution of individual members. One or two students will not help, and the more motivated or capable students do the assignment in order to preserve their own grades. Poor attitudes and friction are the natural result. Some of these difficulties can be solved or avoided by assigning specific roles, as suggested in the previous section. Following this method, along with providing feedback to individuals (using some of the ideas in the next section), can send messages about the importance of cooperation and shared responsibility. Most of these problems usually arise when teachers are unsure of how to assess or provide feedback to students about their work in groups.

In thinking about measuring the learning of mathematical content, the possibilities extend to the limit of the imagination. Johnson and Johnson

(1991) provide some interesting and practical ideas for balancing the evaluation of group and individual work. In addition to observations of the performance of students in groups and interviews with them while they are working together, the following examples offer ways to combine more traditional testing approaches with group work. These approaches assume that students have been working together in groups prior to the assessment procedure.

Individual assessment — group assessment. In this approach, the class is first given an assessment during which students work individually (as is traditionally done). The items can be open-ended, nonroutine tasks or even more traditional test items. Before scoring the individual papers, the teacher makes copies and returns them. Students are placed in groups to retake the test as a group. The group's goal is to make sure that each student understands every question and to hand in a group paper. The teacher can observe the group work to ensure that individuals are contributing.

A standard is set for the group test — for example, 90 percent — and if this is met, individuals in the group get a bonus, say five points, added to their individual score. This is a creative and practical strategy for combining individual and group efforts in assessment. The group standard and the bonus points can be modified for specific situations. Other modifications can be made regarding the composition of the groups, the time allotted, and so forth. This method is especially valuable for tasks that may be open-ended, with several possible solution strategies or answers. The standard for the group paper can include both the percent correct and the number or quality of the solution efforts.

Weekly assessment — final assessment. Another innovative approach suggested by Johnson and Johnson (1991) is weekly evaluation of group work combined with an individual final assessment. Weekly tests are given in which pairs of students work together to complete the test; they agree on answers to produce a single paper between them. Next, each pair joins another one to form a group of four. This group of four typically would be the same that has been working together during the week on learning activities leading up to the test. The four students compare and discuss their papers and produce one paper to hand in, reflecting their group effort. Each member of the group signs the paper verifying that they agree with the answers and that they understand them.

At the end of a grading period, individual students take a "final" exam. If any student scores below a preset criterion score — for example, 80 percent — the four-person group works with the student to review the material until he or she can meet the criterion.

These are just two examples of the many possibilities that can be adapted to balance group and individual contributions in assessment settings. If substantial amounts of time and work are spent in group learning situations, assessment must reflect the contributions and knowledge developed there. Legitimate concerns exist that group assessment alone can interfere with individual mastery. The goal is instead to develop approaches so that group assessments can build and expand individual mastery beyond what it might be traditionally.

Assessing Individual and Group Cooperation and Behavior

As we have seen, in order for a group to work well, each individual member must perform and cooperate. Many teachers are satisfied with very informal approaches to evaluating this behavior; they use simple check marks or even informal mental notes to keep track of how students work. Other teachers wish to build assessments of group cooperation and performance into their overall evaluation plan, providing specific information that can be used for feedback to students and others. This approach may be especially important when developing students' ability to work together and supplying specific feedback on the expected types of behavior. Performance ratings can also be used by students themselves to assess and reflect on their own work in a group; the outcome can be increased self-awareness and responsibility for cooperative work.

Exhibit 8.1 shows an example of the categories that can be used to assess how well an individual member performs in a group. This system can be used in many different ways. It can be a checklist against which a tally is made each time a behavior is observed. It can be the basis for a holistic assessment, in which the teacher records "often," "sometimes," or "seldom." The subcategories, which can simply be descriptors of the types of behaviors a teacher looks for, make it necessary only to record an assessment of the five major categories. Many teachers use a scale of this type, perhaps somewhat simplified, to give to students for self-evaluation or for evaluation of other members of the group.

How can a teacher manage to do this type of assessment while monitoring the work of groups and helping to guide their learning? Many teachers develop approaches that depend on good organization and management. For example, some teachers rotate around the classroom, touching base with each group three or four times during each period and recording an assessment of the group on each visit. Another strategy is to identify a few students during each group activity period for observation and assessment.

These methods can furnish both the teacher and the student with useful information and evaluation. They emphasize to each student that her or his activity within the group is important, and they can provide specific feedback on what students can do to improve their performance within the group. For example, if given a high mark for "getting the group working" or "seriously considering others' ideas," a student is more likely to exhibit that behavior in the future. Students need specific and positive feedback in order to improve their behavior, not only in groups but in other settings. This positive behavior will result in better mathematics learning.

Exhibit 8.1. Performance Rating Sheet.

Names of group members:

_____

_____

_____

_____

Student name _____

  I. Group Participation
     a. Participated in group discussion without prompting
     b. Did his or her fair share of work
     c. Interrupted; tried to dominate
     d. Participated in group's activities
 II. Staying on Topic
     a. Paid attention
     b. Made comments to get group back to the topic
     c. Got off topic
     d. Stayed on the topic
III. Involving Others
     a. Asked questions to involve others; requested input
     b. Tried to get the group working
     c. Seriously considered the ideas of others
     d. Involved others
 IV. Communication
     a. Spoke clearly; was easy to understand
     b. Expressed ideas clearly and effectively
     c. Communicated clearly
  V. Responsibility
     a. Was unreliable; needs encouragement to finish work
     b. Does fair share of the work
     c. Was well prepared

Assessing Mathematical Outcomes

Mathematics content is the focus of group work, but it may be more central on some days than others. For example, if a topic is being reviewed or practiced, it may be possible to concentrate on group performance, giving time and attention to observing and recording processes and interactions. At other times, perhaps when a major concept or procedure is being introduced or applied, it will be critical that the attention is directed toward the individuals' and groups' mathematical performance. Thought and planning must be given to what aspect of group work is most important on a particular day and to what extent it is necessary to assess the group's performance. It is rarely possible to do everything all of the time.

      In assessing the content outcomes, all of the concerns discussed in Chapters Three and Four involving concepts, procedures, and problem solving are applicable. In addition to the task or product that groups produce, it is essential to look at the processes by which they arrived at the outcome. In this case, the mathematical thinking processes of the group are as important as the individuals within it. This assessment goes beyond how students work together and cooperate as group members. It focuses on how well they work in thinking through a mathematical task. The group's work can be assessed through the use of any of the rating forms or rubrics described in Chapter Ten. Figure 8.1 provides an example adapted from Vermont's Mathematics Portfolio Assessment Program (Vermont Department of Education, 1990). Each horizontal line could be a group, and the spaces could be used for tallies or ratings suggested by the criteria at the bottom of the form.

This type of a rating form can be used for each group activity or product, or it can be utilized in conjunction with a group portfolio. This approach may be appropriate if groups stay together for an extended period of time or work on a series of tasks. The group product can also be selected by any of the individual members for their portfolio, as an example of group work.

Most teachers and students feel more comfortable with a combination group and individual assessment of mathematical achievement. There are many ways to accomplish this, depending on the class and on the content learning that is being assessed. One method is to use a rating such as the one just given for each individual's contribution. Since this is probably too time-consuming, an alternative is to have each member write a summary of the work done by the group. Another simple approach is to follow the group activity with an assessment task — a quiz, homework, or a problem similar to that done by the group — completed individually and independently. Each member of the group will then feel responsible for understanding the content before the group's report is complete. Some teachers suggest allowing students to select the problems to be graded, whether from the group assignment or the individual task.

Group work and its assessment are complex. Teachers look for and value many different aspects of group work, both regarding the content being learned and the quality of the group interactions. One teacher commented, "When I use group work, I look for encouraging words." Another said, "I decide what is important in a lesson, and upon reflection I may change the focus depending on the lesson. Over a period of time, the desired behaviors will occur." Another teacher stated, "After group work, I assess individuals based on what was done in class. I may give a topic quiz. The group is a context where they learn the content. However, I do this only if I am sure that the groups coalesce and know the content." Another said, "I'm looking for them to be able to explain whatever it is they are doing in an articulate manner connected with previous learning. Everybody can talk." Another reported, "I look for consensus. Everybody comes up with an idea."

The suggestions and strategies given here are intended to guide this type of holistic assessment and also to make it clear to both teachers and students that group work is important and worth evaluating on the basis of mutually understood criteria.

Figure 8.1. Sample Rating Form.

Understanding of task	Quality of approaches/procedures	Decisions along the way	Outcomes of activities	Language of mathematics	Mathematical representation	Clarity of presentation
1. Totally misunderstood 2. Partially understood 3. Understood 4. Extended	1. Inappropriate 2. Appropriate some of the time 3. Workable 4. Efficient or sophisticated	1. No evidence of reasoning 2. Reasoned decision making possible 3. Reasoned decisions inferred 4. Reasoned decisions shown	1. Solutions without extensions 2. Solutions with observations 3. Solutions with connections 4. Solutions with synthesis, generally	1. No use of math language 2. Appropriate use some of the time 3. Appropriate use most of the time 4. Use of rich, precise, elegant math language	1. No use of math representations 2. Use of math representations 3. Accurate and appropriate use of math representations 4. Perceptive use of math representations	1. Unclear 2. Some clear parts 3. Mostly clear 4. Clear; well organized; complete

9

STUDENT SELF-ASSESSMENT
AND AFFECTIVE FACTORS

RESEARCH HAS SUGGESTED THAT STUDENTS WHO ARE ABLE TO EVALUATE THEIR
own thinking and learning processes have higher achievement. This is called
metacognition, or thinking about thinking. Students can develop metacognitive ability for self-checking by participating in the types of alternative
assessment activities discussed so far. Another by-product of these assessment strategies is that students' feelings about mathematics are improved.
Methods such as projects, investigations, and portfolios, integrated with instruction, seem less like tests and more like the kinds of engaging, motivating activities that students learn from every day.

Metacognition, Beliefs, and Problem Solving

Metacognition is an important part of any learning process, but it is especially essential in problem solving and other similar higher-order thinking
activities. According to Flavell (1976), *metacognition* refers to the active monitoring and consequent regulation and organization of these processes and
to the cognitive objects on which they bear. When students are asked to analyze their problem-solving processes, there is a measurable effect on performance (Schoenfeld, 1983). Students base the way they think about their
mathematical abilities on their beliefs and attitudes about mathematics. By
helping students look accurately at their own mathematical thinking processes, we can enhance awareness of their abilities and improve their feelings toward the subject.

Schoenfeld (1983) suggests that there are three categories of knowledge and behavior required for problem solving. One category includes
resources, such as facts and algorithms, routine procedures, and heuristic
knowledge needed to solve the problem at hand. The second category, control, involves the selection and implementation of available cognitive resources. Control processes include activities like monitoring, assessment,

decision making, and conscious metacognitive acts. Finally, problem solving involves a third category, belief systems, which encompass the individual's mathematical world view — the perspectives with which one approaches mathematics and mathematical tasks. These are beliefs dealing with self, the environment, the topic, and mathematics. Each of these processes is important, and each must work in concert with the others in higher-order thinking.

A very familiar example to teachers is one in which students have the procedural knowledge, such as knowing the operations of adding or multiplying, but lack the heuristic resources or the decision-making control processes that help decide which operation should be used for which situation. Another typical situation is work by students who begin to solve a problem by performing computations and trying various approaches without pausing to think about whether their approach will lead toward the final solution. In this situation, resources are available that could lead to a solution, but monitoring and control processes are either missing or not engaged. Two other examples illustrate the importance of belief systems. The first is the case in which students may be unable to solve a nonroutine problem or deal with an unfamiliar context or application. As we have seen, many students develop strong beliefs about the nature of mathematics. They believe there is one way to do something and that if they have not seen or practiced a problem or procedure, they cannot be expected to do it. A second area of beliefs has to do with the motivation to try or to persist on a more difficult task that requires thinking and reasoning.

In the mathematics classroom, belief systems often clash. The teacher's belief system may, for example, be built upon success in mathematics leading to the notion that it is important and the way to learn it is through drill and practice. The students may not have a strong awareness of their own beliefs but may think that mathematics has very limited usefulness and is certainly not relevant to their own daily lives. These beliefs provide the context in which the students respond to mathematical activities, including the selection and use of resources and strategies. Without positive attitudes and beliefs, students have very little chance of developing higher-order thinking abilities.

Awareness of Beliefs and Attitudes

What do these ideas about metacognition and beliefs have to do with alternative assessment? Since beliefs shape attitudes and emotions and direct the decisions during mathematical activity, it is reasonable to conclude that the more students are aware of the factors that drive their behavior, the more potential there is for changing that behavior for the better. Unlike traditional tests, many alternative assessment tasks can create an opportunity for a teacher to become aware of students' attitudes; this can open the door to helping students see how these attitudes affect their performance. In examining and evaluating student work on assessment tasks, the teacher can be a diagnostician, interpreting the students' work mathematically but also drawing information about their control processes and belief systems.

As a first step toward thinking about student work as reflections of attitudes, we will look at some examples of student work and try to interpret how the student may feel about doing mathematics and also how the student views it.

Figure 9.1. Concert Stage.

Vanilla Ice has hired you to design the stage for the next concert. The stage should be rectangular, and have an area of 1,000 square feet. It will have a security rope on both sides and the front. Make some drawings of different rectangles that have 1,000 square feet of area. How many feet of security rope is needed for each one? Which shape would you use? Why?

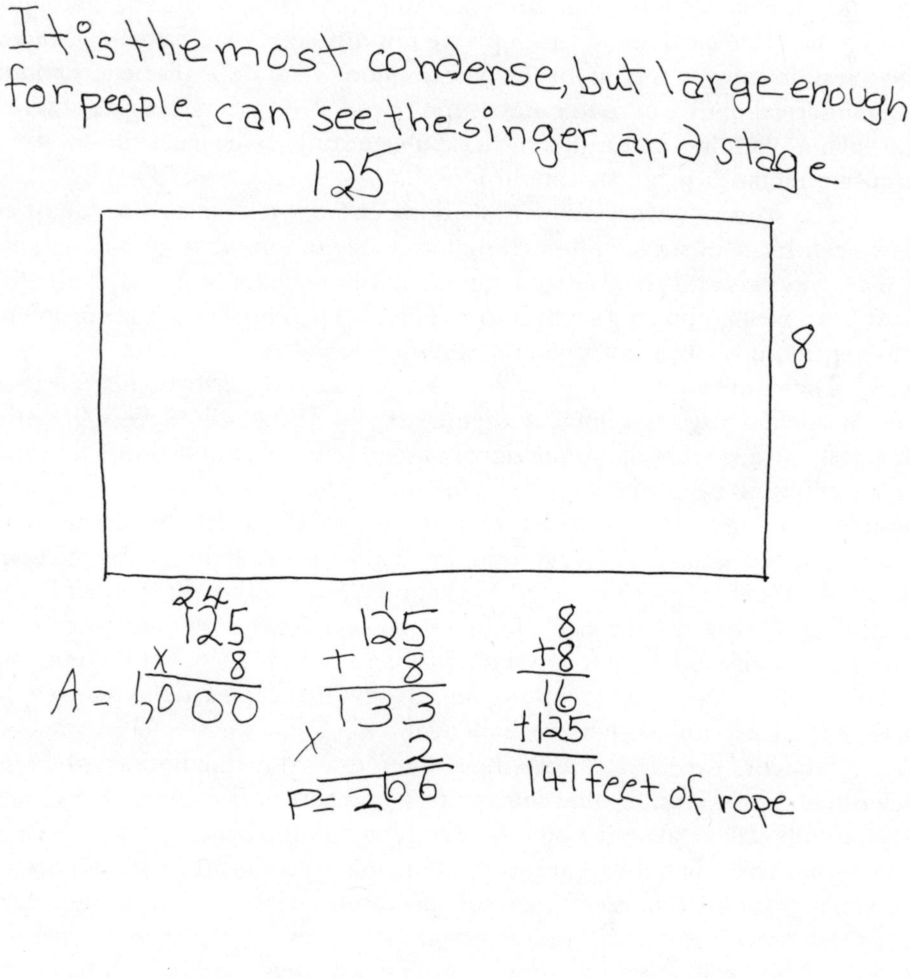

It is the most condense, but large enough for people can see the singer and stage

125

$$A = 1,000$$

$$\begin{array}{r} 125 \\ \times\ \ 8 \\ \hline 1,000 \end{array}$$

$$\begin{array}{r} 125 \\ +\ \ 8 \\ \hline 133 \\ \times\ \ 2 \\ \hline P = 266 \end{array}$$

$$\begin{array}{r} 8 \\ +8 \\ \hline 16 \\ +125 \\ \hline 141 \end{array}$$ feet of rope

The picture and the calculation in Figure 9.1, which we saw in Chapter Six, suggest that the student may have a "recipe" approach to problem solving. However, the student provided an extended answer that is relevant to the question, giving evidence that there is a positive attitude toward mathematical thinking in relevant, applied situations.

Figure 9.2 is an interesting example we saw in Chapter Seven. In looking at this paper from a belief systems' point of view, we can readily see that the student lacks persistence and has no desire to do the problem. Yet the student uses symbols in communicating this attitude — an arrow symbol to mean "up." The student did a good job of drawing a rectangle and has used the concept of reflection about a line of symmetry. This may tell us the student is a geometric thinker and simply does not like this type of problem, which uses mainly arithmetic. At first glance, this does seem to be a student with a poor attitude; yet with some interpretation, it may be more a case of lack of ability to control and apply available knowledge to this task.

The answer and tidiness of the work in Figure 9.3 may indicate that the student believes it is the nature of mathematics to be neat and to follow rules. The numerical answer is of prime importance to the student, though the question calls for a plan for the painting job. This student's beliefs about the numerical nature of mathematics may be so strong that the idea of writing such a plan does not fit his or her expectations about what the solution to a mathematics problem should look like.

The student's work shown in Figure 9.4, which we saw in Chapter Two, exhibits a positive approach that goes beyond making the mathematical calculations and generating a complete list of needed supplies. This student has a well-connected set of resources and control processes for problem solving, along with a positive and well-developed belief system.

The connection among beliefs, attitudes, and performance is complex and changing. At times, students may feel they will be unsuccessful at a task because they have previously failed at similar questions, producing a self-fulfilling prophecy. Performance is affected by beliefs; a student who feels that mathematics must be memorized will be hindered when the terms and procedures are forgotten. The student who believes that mathematics is created and constructed can reproduce or derive the needed information and be more successful. Beliefs can also influence not only the selection and use of methods for solving a problem but the motivation for doing a task at all. Is the student finding an answer just to please the teacher, to satisfy curiosity, or to meet a challenge?

Students' experiences form their beliefs toward mathematics and themselves. These determine what information and concepts they think are relevant to a problem. As previously stated, change in mathematical behavior can be positive when awareness of these beliefs occurs. Students can arrive at the realization that their methods are appropriate and that their self-checking processes will aid them to become successful at mathematical activities. This realization can reduce mathematical anxiety, which has been

Figure 9.2. Kathy's Dog Pen.

Kathy is building a pen for her dog. She has 64 feet of fencing and wants to build it in the shape of a rectangle. Make some drawings of rectangles that Kathy could make that would use all 64 feet of the fence. Which one of these rectangles do you think she should build? Why?

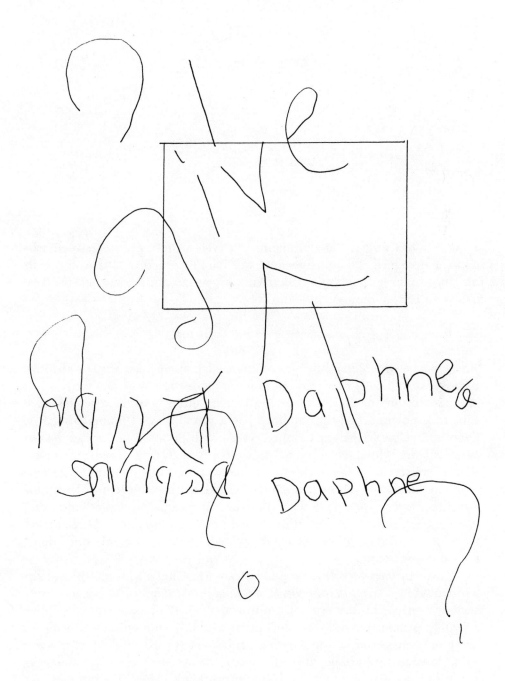

Figure 9.3. Luke's Room.

Luke wants to paint one wall of his room. The wall is 20 feet wide and 8 feet high. It takes one can of paint to cover 80 square feet, and the paint is sold at $4.99 a can. What else does Luke need to think of? Make a plan for Luke's trip to the store for supplies for this painting job.

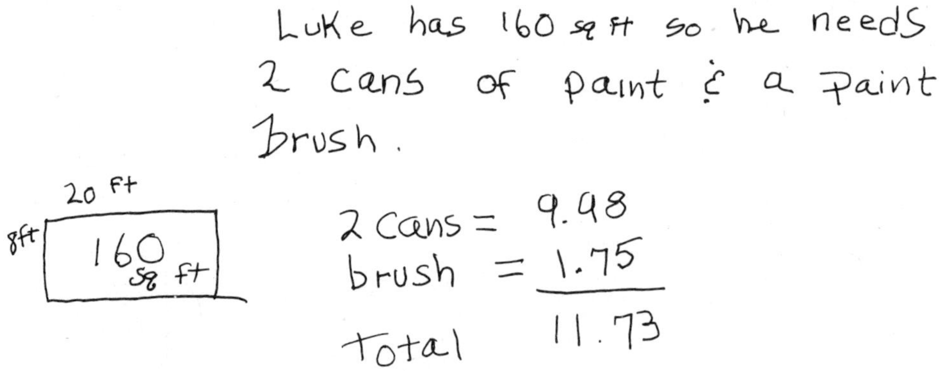

Luke has 160 sq ft so he needs 2 cans of paint & a paint brush.

20 ft
8ft [160 sq ft]

2 cans = 9.98
brush = 1.75
total   11.73

shown to affect students' achievement negatively. Alternative assessment can help teachers have some insight into this complex picture. It is difficult to imagine anything more important in teaching than understanding students' beliefs and motivations about the subject.

Assessing Metacognition

Many teachers have good, informal knowledge about their students' thinking processes. They know that one student tends to be very methodical and careful, that another has a creative flair and often finds unexpected solutions to problems, and that another has a visual way of doing problems. These are valuable insights, gained through observation and awareness of students' work. However, it is often difficult, especially from traditional homework exercises, worksheets, and tests, to see how students think. The emphasis in the mathematics curriculum on standard procedures and algorithms sometimes forces students to "hide" their own individual strategies for finding answers and solutions. By the time students enter the middle and high school years, many of them have become convinced that there is only one "right" way of doing mathematics.

Student-centered instructional strategies, along with alternative assessment tasks, can open windows to students' thinking processes, give positive feedback on useful and creative approaches, and help students who have difficulty. To illustrate how simple, open-ended tasks can reveal the metacognitive processes used by students, we again look at some samples of student work. We can see various types of evidence of self-awareness and metacognition as students monitor their solution processes. The three samples also show increasingly subtle indications of metacognition. In the first one, the

Figure 9.4. Luke's Room.

Luke wants to paint one wall of his room. The wall is 20 feet wide and 8 feet high. It takes one can of paint to cover 80 square feet, and the paint is sold at $4.99 a can. What else does Luke need to think of? Make a plan for Luke's trip to the store for supplies for this painting job.

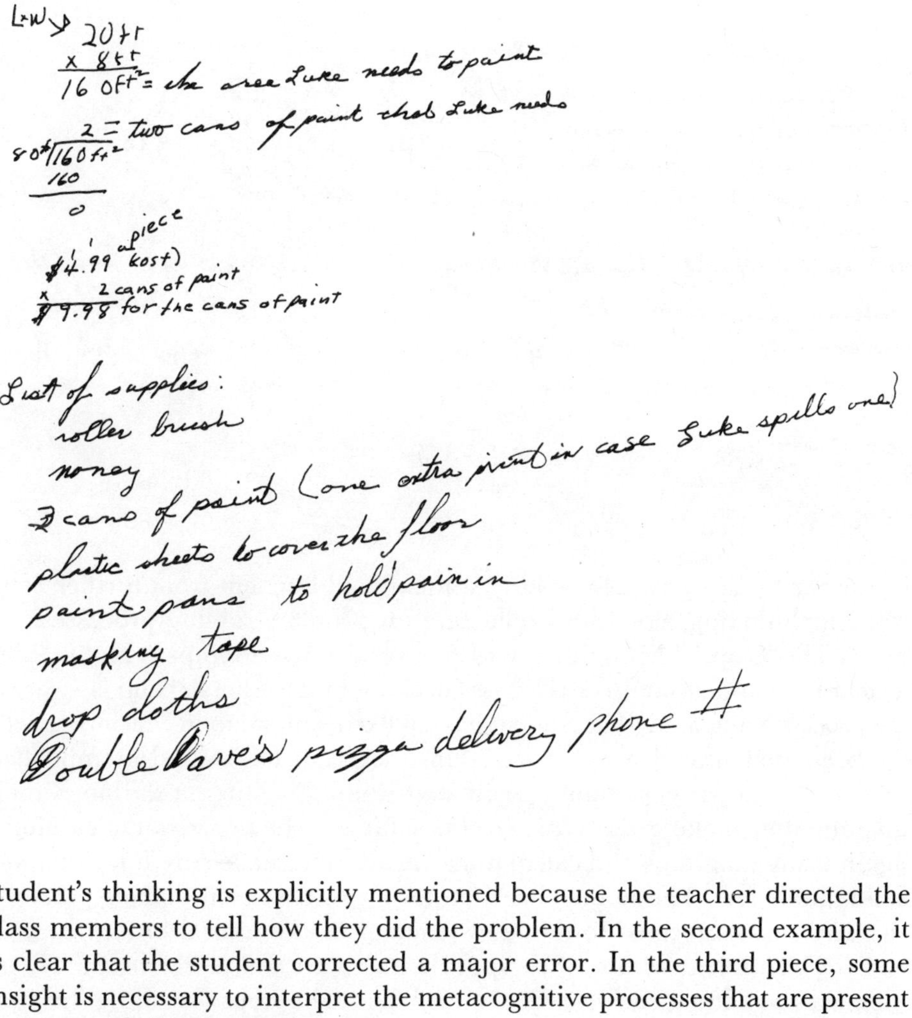

L×W→ 20 ft
$\quad$ × 8 ft
$\quad$ 16 0 ft² = the area Luke needs to paint

$\quad$ 2 = two cans of paint that Luke needs
80⁾‾160 ft²
160
‾‾‾‾
$\quad$ 0

$4.99 apiece (cost)
× 2 cans of paint
$9.98 for the cans of paint

List of supplies:
roller brush
money
2 cans of paint (one extra paint in case Luke spills one)
plastic sheets to cover the floor
paint pans to hold paint in
masking tape
drop cloths
Double Dave's pizza delivery phone #

student's thinking is explicitly mentioned because the teacher directed the class members to tell how they did the problem. In the second example, it is clear that the student corrected a major error. In the third piece, some insight is necessary to interpret the metacognitive processes that are present and at work for the student.

The student whose work is shown in Figure 9.5 is thinking about her or his thinking. "Logic" is the student's way of trying to describe something that is going on as he or she uses the times tables and other mathematical knowledge to develop steps toward a solution. The student seems to be aware that something other than the mathematical knowledge itself is a part of the thinking process. A continual monitoring process is in place, indicated by the "why, logic" comments at the end of each step. The final sentence, "I know how to do this thing, although I don't know why I'm doing this," shows that the student has become aware that logic is not enough to describe what

Figure 9.5. Luke's Room.

Luke wants to paint one wall of his room. The wall is 20 feet wide and 8 feet high. It takes one can of paint to cover 80 square feet, and the paint is sold at $4.99 a can. What else does Luke need to think of? Make a plan for Luke's trip to the store for supplies for this painting job.

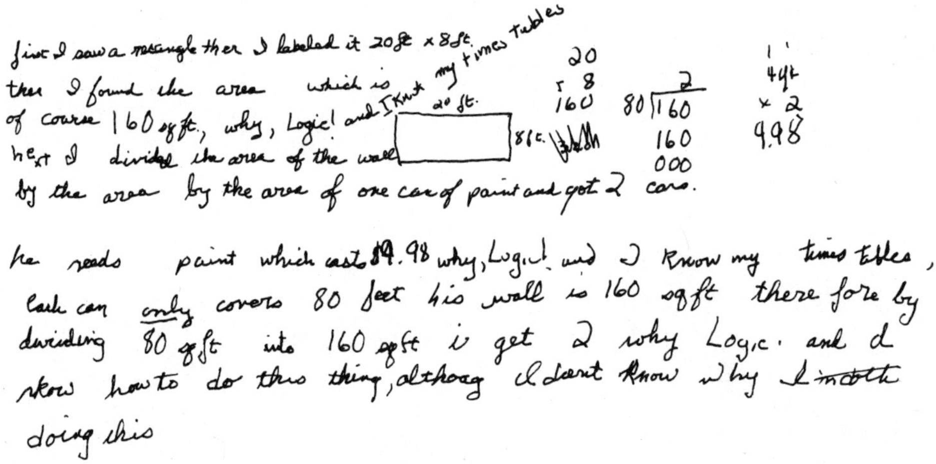

his or her thinking is. This young student could benefit from further occasions for thinking aloud and reflecting on problem-solving processes.

The "Oops!!! Mess up!!!" written over the first attempt in Figure 9.6 is a clear indication that this student is checking him- or herself and is aware of the process being used. The student has circled the diagram in which perimeter has been used instead of area in designing the stage. The second attempt offers evidence of persistence and a positive attitude; the student did not simply give up after making an error. In this solution, she or he works carefully, again using diagrams and calculating the areas to make sure it is one thousand square feet. The student has monitoring and decision-making processes that are well-connected to the knowledge of mathematical procedures.

The student whose work appears in Figure 9.7 works in a fairly organized way, doing each step in the problem. The steps of finding the area, calculating the cost of paint, and writing the plan are delineated by lines; these show a sense of doing each part and going on to the next. The check mark is an indication that the student finished that part and checked it before doing the next aspect of the problem. Crossing out the division of 80 by 4.99 indicates clearly that the student has monitored his or her thinking and is aware of using the appropriate operation. Finally, the student writes an answer that justifies the connections between the steps. This small piece of work gives strong evidence that the student has a well-developed and active set of control and decision-making processes in place and is able to use them in solving a problem.

Figure 9.6. Concert Stage.

Vanilla Ice has hired you to design the stage for the next concert. The stage should be rectangular, and have an area of 1,000 square feet. It will have a security rope on both sides and the front. Make some drawings of different rectangles that have 1,000 square feet of area. How many feet of security rope is needed for each one? Which shape would you use? Why?

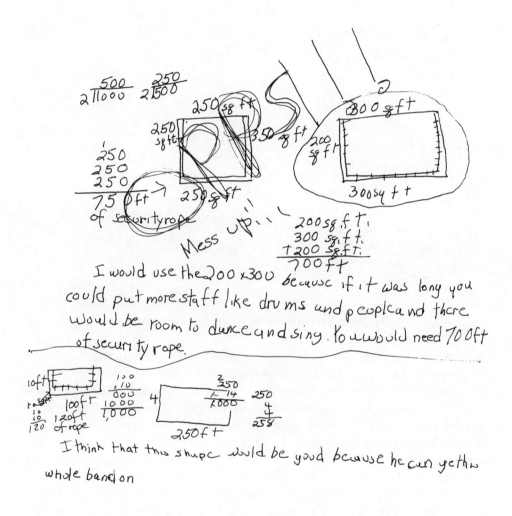

I would use the 200 x 300 because if it was long you could put more staff like drums and people and there would be room to dance and sing. You would need 700ft of security rope.

I think that this shape would be good because he can get the whole band on

The development and use by students of their metacognitive processes should not be expected to happen by accident or allowed to happen only incidentally. Explicit opportunities during mathematics instruction, along with feedback based on assessment tasks, can help these important processes develop. Research has shown that mathematical knowledge alone is not sufficient to ensure the development of higher-order thinking and problem-solving abilities.

Figure 9.7. Luke's Room.

Luke wants to paint one wall of his room. The wall is 20 feet wide and 8 feet high. It takes one can of paint to cover 80 square feet, and the paint is sold at $4.99 a can. What else does Luke need to think of? Make a plan for Luke's trip to the store for supplies for this painting job.

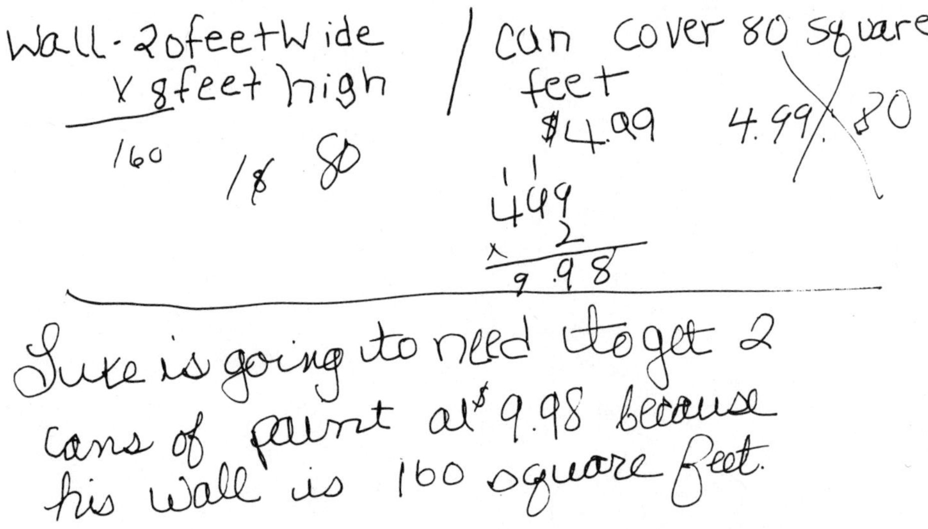

Wall - 20 feet Wide
    x 8 feet high

160   18   80

1 can cover 80 square feet
$4.99   4.99 x 80

$$4\overset{1}{\underset{}{9}}\overset{1}{9}$$
$$\times \quad 2$$
$$\overline{9.98}$$

Luke is going to need to get 2 cans of paint at $9.98 because his wall is 160 square feet.

Student Self-Assessment of Performance

The techniques of authentic assessment, integrated with instruction, have the potential to change the beliefs students have about mathematics. Two key processes in alternative assessment can involve students and help them develop heightened awareness of their own thinking processes and mathematical strengths or areas needing improvement. The first strategy is getting students to help develop scoring rubrics and then to evaluate their own work using the rubric. The second important strategy is using portfolios as a context for students to select their work.

    Details about rubric development and students' role in the process are provided in Chapter Ten. The primary points to think of in relation to self-assessment include the development of the rubric and students' use of it in reflecting on their own work. Developing a rubric can be a learning experience that is just as helpful as doing assessment tasks themselves. Setting clear expectations for performance is essential for effective instruction and learning. The rubric, along with prototypes of student work that meets high standards, can serve this purpose. For example, consider the following statement of exemplary performance from the California Assessment Program (Stenmark, 1989, p. 19): "Gives a complete response with a clear, coherent, unambiguous, and elegant explanation; includes a clear and simplified diagram, communicates effectively to the identified audience, shows understanding of the open-ended problems' mathematical ideas and processes; identifies all important elements of the problem, may include examples and counter examples, presents strong supportive arguments."

Although the specific language and terminology might be adapted to students' grade level, this statement sets out high expectations and identifies the kind of performance needed to receive an exemplary rating. If a student is provided feedback and spends some time comparing his or her own responses to this criterion, a great deal of reflection and awareness can take place.

Portfolios can play a significant role in helping students develop their own standards and self-assessment. We know that portfolios develop the attributes of self-checking by helping the students focus on their work. As they go through their assignments, either individually or with a teacher or parent, students learn to ask questions that focus on the quality of the work they have done. Is this piece better than this one? How did I solve that problem? Is my work improving? As a result of identifying standards and judging their own work, students become aware of their mathematical abilities. The portfolio provides multiple reflections of these abilities so that successes can be seen and individual strengths identified.

By reflecting on individual assessment tasks with the guidance of rubrics and by selecting their best work for a portfolio, students become engaged in their mathematical learning. One of the most difficult challenges in school mathematics is to develop students' sense of involvement in meaningful and relevant work. The combination of student-centered and problem-oriented instruction with assessment that brings students into the process can help to meet this challenge.

Developing the ability and habit of self-checking is a difficult task. Miller (1992) reports that students are reluctant to answer questions about their work in writing, whether in a group, with a partner, or with the whole class. It is important to use questions consistently during instruction — for example, what did you like about the piece? What were you thinking about? What is done well there? What needs to be improved?

Students do not naturally think of their work in this manner. They have always had someone like parents, teachers, or coaches to judge their performance. The belief that someone else will tell them how good they are at writing or mathematics is a significant hurdle to overcome. The idea of analyzing their own work is a very new and unique experience to most students. Yet the result of this type of training is that students learn to evaluate themselves, to take responsibility for their learning, to track their judgment, and to develop a self-critical capacity.

Student Journals

In as well as out of school, mathematics teachers encounter statements such as "You are a math teacher? I always hated math!" These comments reflect the attitude that many people, including parents and colleagues, have about mathematics. They have developed the belief that it is an abstract, boring, and difficult discipline. As a result, many people avoid courses and careers that involve mathematics or science.

Students tend to withdraw or make overt negative comments during class, which can cause friction with the teacher so that he or she ignores the students or punishes them. The result, of course, is further negative behavior and worse attitudes. If a teacher is aware of and becomes concerned about student attitudes, these can be improved using alternative assessment techniques blended with instruction.

Student journals are an effective tool for accomplishing the dual objectives of assessing attitudes and focusing on mathematical thinking. The goal of assessment using journals should be to reveal and monitor students' attitudes and thinking. Evaluation should be a secondary goal for teachers, who may only give a check mark or other indication of completion, rather than rate or score the students' efforts.

One of the most typical and useful approaches to journals is to ask students to write and reflect on the processes and thinking they use in solving a problem or learning a concept. Even young children can learn to do this type of writing, especially if the first attempts are structured and if the teacher reacts positively to what students write. Some teachers find that having students respond to questions helps them open up and reveal their thinking. Students respond to questions such as "I liked this problem because . . . " or "This problem reminded me of . . . " or "The hardest part of this problem was . . . " Writing about problems not only reveals attitudes and interests but is effective in helping students develop an awareness of their thinking strategies and their mathematical knowledge.

A second important approach is based on the more traditional idea of what a journal is: that is, a long-term log or record in which students regularly write about mathematics class, learning, and related personal thoughts and experiences. Depending on the individual student, this type of journal can be very personal. A good deal of judgment must be used in considering how to use this sort of journal. It can be a very effective way for students to communicate their beliefs and attitudes to the teacher, if there is mutual trust. It may be a good idea to allow the student to decide which parts of the journal to share with the teacher. An effective strategy is to provide specific questions or topics from time to time for students to include in their journal, making it clear that these will be read by the teacher. Openers can be used to focus the writing: "The best (worst) thing about math class this week was . . . " or "The thing I do (don't) understand about congruent triangles is . . . " or "In math, I am really good at . . . "

The NCTM *Standards* stresses the importance of mathematical communications. Writing about mathematics—how it is learned and what is difficult about it—is an excellent way for students to develop abilities in communication. Teachers who use journals as a component of their assessment program are unanimous in saying that students learn something about their own attitudes and mathematical thinking. Teachers also report that the improvement in students' writing is significant. Elementary teachers see this writing skill carried over into other subjects. Writing in mathematics can help focus on thinking and reasoning. Students and teachers can work together on the idea that thinking is what mathematics is all about.

10

SCORING AND
GRADING TECHNIQUES

A KEY COMPONENT OF MANY ALTERNATIVE ASSESSMENT APPROACHES IS THE use of a range of procedures for assigning scores to students' work. Most scoring approaches use variations of "holistic" scoring. Holistic scoring breaks with the traditional method of grading based upon the number of correct items and goes beyond merely providing partial credit for solutions that are not complete or have errors.

Holistic scoring is an invaluable tool when evaluating problem-solving or other higher-order thinking processes. The procedure allows the teacher to gauge the overall quality of the responses and the level of thinking demonstrated by the students (Pandey, 1991). As a result, the teacher gains further insight into the students' level of understanding when performing certain tasks. It is also possible to evaluate the quality of students' approaches, procedures, and strategies, which are the necessary components of problem solving. Holistic scoring makes it possible to track the choices made by students as they solve a problem. Finally, this kind of scoring can include an assessment of the decisions made: the reasons students made those decisions, their observations and conclusions, the connections to other mathematical topics or subjects, and any generalizations the students reached.

Scoring Rubrics

An important procedure implementing holistic scoring is designing a rubric that helps standardize and guide the scoring procedure. A *rubric* is a framework that can be designed or adapted by the teacher for a particular group of students or mathematical tasks. The design of a rubric can provide an excellent opportunity to involve students, giving them a chance to identify the thinking and learning processes they and the teacher think are important criteria for scoring and grading. Once the design is done, the categories are subdivided and scored using a numerical scale. We will look at examples

from the California Mathematics Council's open-ended questions rubric
(Stenmark, 1989), the Vermont Mathematics Portfolio Assessment Program
(1990), the Maryland Performance Assessment Program (1992), and others.

Here is an example of a simple rubric used by Beth Douglass, a geometry teacher:

Understanding the Problem
4 points—Complete understanding
2 points—Some difficulty
1 point—Poor understanding

Solution
4 points—Correct solution
2 points—Almost correct
1 point—Attempt

Explanation
4 points—Complete explanation
2 points—Incomplete explanation
1 point—Poor explanation

Douglass decided to focus on three main processes in problem solving. Her students could see that showing an understanding of the problem
and giving an explanation were each as important as the solution itself. They
also knew that understanding the problem, giving a complete explanation,
and providing a solution that was almost correct would be worth ten out
of the possible twelve points. This rubric makes it very clear to students what
the teacher thinks is most important for them to learn. Even this simple rubric
is very rich in its ability to communicate expectations to students and in
its flexibility in assigning a score to the solution of a problem.

General or Holistic Rubrics

One key decision to make is whether to focus on a mathematical process,
such as problem solving, communication, reasoning, or proving. An alternative is to use a general (holistic) rubric that can apply to any mathematical
process or topic. General rubrics are often used on national or state assessments or on others that must take into account a broad range of mathematical tasks and students. The rubric used by the California Mathematics Council (Stenmark, 1989) is a good example (see Exhibit 10.1).

Notice that this general rubric is aimed at assigning an overall score
rather than a score for particular processes. This type of rubric is appropriate for assessments that are more summative, such as major tests or exami-
nations. It does not provide a great deal of specific feedback to the teacher
or student about the processes or mathematics content that might need further attention or instruction. Nevertheless, this rubric does make it possible

Exhibit 10.1. The California Mathematics Council's Rubric for Open-Ended Questions.

Demonstrated Competence
Exemplary response (6 points) — Gives a complete response with a clear, coherent, unambiguous, and elegant explanation; includes a clear and simplified diagram, communicates effectively to the identified audience, shows understanding of the open-ended problems' mathematical ideas and processes, identifies all important elements of the problem, may include examples and counter examples, presents strong supportive arguments

Competent response (5 points) — Gives a fairly complete response, fairly clear explanations, includes an appropriate diagram, communicates effectively, shows understanding of the problem's mathematical ideas and processes, identifies the most important elements of the problem, presents a solid argument

Satisfactory Response
Minor flaws (4 points) — Satisfactorily completes the problem, a muddled explanation, incomplete argumentation, diagram unclear or inappropriate, understands underlying mathematical ideas, uses mathematical ideas effectively

Serious flaws (3 points) — Began problem appropriately, failed to complete it, omitted significant parts, failed to show full understanding of mathematical ideas and processes, major computational errors, misuse or lack of use of mathematical terms, used an inappropriate strategy

Inadequate Response
Begins but fails to complete problem (2 points) — Cannot understand explanation, unclear diagram, shows no understanding of the problem situation, major computational errors

Unable to begin (1 point) — Inappropriate explanation, diagram misrepresents the problem, copies problem but no attempt at a solution, fails to identify appropriate information

No attempt (0 points)

---

to assess large groups of students validly and reliably on open-ended and nonroutine tasks.

The descriptions of each score are precise enough so that in a short time teachers or other persons can be trained to use the scoring scale with high levels of agreement and reliability. Although most teachers do not necessarily write out the descriptions of their own scales formally, they do have a good idea of what each score means. It is also important to communicate to students the meaning of a score. They should know, for example, what a four means on a scale that measures their understanding of a problem. Discussions of these criteria can themselves provide an excellent opportunity for teachers and students to explore key issues — for example, what it means to understand a problem or what "correctness" of a solution might involve, beyond a simple answer.

Anaholistic Rubrics

A student's paper can be rated on more than one criterion, with the possibility of summing the scores to obtain a total. DeStefano (1993) has used the term *anaholistic* to describe this type of approach, as opposed to a holistic measurement in which one generalized rubric is used to assign a single score to the paper. Anaholistic approaches generally provide more information about a task and furnish different perspectives. They pinpoint strengths and weaknesses, allowing the students and teacher to recognize areas for further work. The process rubrics discussed in the next section can be scored anaholistically to create a profile of the development of problem-solving, reasoning, and communication processes.

Another important use of anaholistic scoring is on students' overall conceptual, problem-solving, and procedural knowledge. These are centerpieces of mathematics education and can be assessed for nearly any type of mathematical task. Here are examples of rubrics that could be used to assess these three important areas; they have been adapted from the Oregon Four-Trait Analytical Scoring Model (Arter, 1993).

Procedural knowledge: evidence of procedural knowledge is provided by the ability to select and apply procedures correctly. Procedural knowledge includes numerical algorithms and operations, as well as the abilities to read and produce graphs and tables, perform geometric constructions and drawings, and perform skills such as rounding and ordering. Finally, it includes being able to justify and verify a procedure using concrete models or other representations and being able to extend or modify procedures when necessary.

> 1 point — Incorrect use of procedures and operations or presence of major errors; little indication of knowing reasons for procedural steps
>
> 2 points — Appropriate use of procedures and operations with only minor errors; some ability to explain or represent procedures
>
> 3 points — Correct use of procedures and operations without errors; able to represent procedures and explain how they work
>
> 4 points — Extended use of procedures and operations; able to show different explanations and reasons for steps; able to extend, adapt, or invent new procedures

Conceptual understanding: evidence of conceptual understanding is provided by the ability to read and interpret mathematical language by making connections between situations, relevant information, and results. Conceptual understanding includes the ability to interrelate models, diagrams, and other representations of concepts; compare and contrast related concepts; and interpret the assumptions and relations involving concepts.

> 1 point — Wide gaps in conceptual understanding; major misconceptions; little or no use of terminology, diagrams, or symbols to represent concepts; lack of conceptual understanding of associated mathematical procedures

2 points — Some gaps in conceptual knowledge or some evidence of misconceptions; models, diagrams, and symbols for representing concepts attempted with some translation from one mode to another; mathematical procedures appropriately used, but with errors, indicating possible weakness in conceptual understanding

3 points — Evidence of conceptual understanding with few gaps or misconceptions; accurate use of models, diagrams, and symbols with evidence of translation from one mode to the other; some recognition of the meaning and interpretation of concepts and associated procedures

4 points — Evidence of understanding and use of concepts; extended use of models, diagrams, and symbols with broad translation from one mode to another; strong evidence of a recognition of the meaning and interpretation of concepts

Problem solving: evidence of problem solving is provided by the ability to interpret a problem and select appropriate information to find a solution strategy. Student uses planning, heuristics, reasoning, and strategic thinking to understand, plan, carry out, and explain the solution to routine, non-routine, and applied problems.

1 point — Unworkable approach; incorrect or no use of mathematical representations; poor use of estimation; lack of understanding

2 points — Appropriate approach, estimation, and implementation of a strategy; possibly reasoned decision making; solution with observations

3 points — Workable approach; estimation and mathematical representation used effectively; reasoned decision making inferred; reasonable solution

4 points — Efficient/sophisticated approach; estimation used effectively; extensive use of mathematical representations; explicit reasoned decision making; solutions with connections, synthesis, or abstraction

Anaholistic rubrics can be used to score either individual or group work. They can also be developed to focus on types of knowledge, such as the Oregon model just described, or on mathematical topics and processes. The following example is from the Connecticut Common Core of Learning Mathematics Assessment program (Baron, 1992). It rates mathematical skills in calculation and estimation; comprehension of the specific mathematical topics of measurement and number; and use of the processes of reasoning, problem solving, communications, and connections. This rubric provides a comprehensive rating of a broad range of mathematical learning.

Mathematical Skills	*Rating*

Calculation/estimation: compute with integers, decimals; use a calculator to compute with large numbers

4 — proficient
3 — adequate
2 — marginal
1 — unsatisfactory

Key Mathematical Understanding	*Rating*

Measurement: estimate; make and use measurements to describe phenomena

4 — thoroughly developed
3 — partially developed
2 — minimally developed
1 — not developed

Number: understand, represent, and use numbers in a variety of forms

4 — thoroughly developed
3 — partially developed
2 — minimally developed
1 — not developed

Critical Process Understanding	*Rating*

Reasoning: use concepts and operations logically, appropriately

4 — thoroughly evident
3 — substantially evident
2 — partially evident
1 — minimally evident

Problem solving: with a variety of representations that enhance understanding

4 — exemplary
3 — effective
2 — marginal
1 — unsuccessful

Connections: implicitly or explicitly connect multiple representations; show threads of reasoning that tie the calculations to larger issues

4 — substantially connected
3 — partially connected
2 — minimally connected
1 — not connected

Communication: convey findings and understandings

4 — exemplary
3 — effective
2 — marginal
1 — unsuccessful

These rubrics can be used over a long-term period to develop a profile of students' mathematical learning, monitoring growth and progress. Although this kind of rubric can be used for providing direct feedback to the student, it can be an even more valuable tool for the teacher.

Because of the time and effort involved, anaholistic approaches (in which a paper or other piece of work is scored on two or more separate scales) are often reserved for major, summative evaluations. They can be useful, for example, in evaluating student portfolios since an individual piece of work might reflect many different types of knowledge.

Process Rubrics

One of the major uses of alternative assessments is to provide opportunities to assess and provide information for teachers and students about mathematical processes such as reasoning, understanding problems, communicating, planning, and decision making. Rubrics that are designed to rate and provide feedback on these processes are of the greatest importance for classrooms. A good process rubric should provide a description of the characteristics of each level of response so that reasonable, qualitative judgments can be made of student work. The following example, adapted from the Maryland School Performance Assessment Program (1992), can be used to assess mathematics tasks from the perspective of communication and reasoning processes.

Communication
3 points — Uses mathematical language (terms, symbols, signs, and/or representations) that is highly effective, accurate, and thorough to describe operations, concepts, and processes

2 points — Uses mathematical language that is partially effective, accurate, and thorough enough to describe operations, concepts, and processes

1 point — Uses mathematical language that is minimally effective and accurate in describing operations, concepts, and processes

Reasoning
3 points — Effectively, accurately, and thoroughly makes predictions and justifies conclusions using information from his or her work

2 points — Is partially effective, accurate, and thorough in making predictions and justifying conclusions using information from his or her work

1 point — Attempts to make predictions and justify conclusions using information from his or her work

Ranging from effective to partial to making an attempt, the levels of this rubric are very simple. This type of approach to separating the levels of response gives greater reliability among raters. It can also be simple enough for students to understand. Yet it does not differentiate a great deal, so that many papers that use quite different types of reasoning may receive a score of two, indicating partial success. Ease in scoring and rating must always be balanced with the amount of information that a rubric can supply to students and the teacher.

In this kind of process rubric, each paper is rated on each process, and a profile consisting of separate scores is produced. These scores are sometimes summed to give a total process score. In classroom use, however, it is better to keep the scores separate until the end of a grading period. In this way, a teacher can evaluate progress on the individual processes.

Another approach to developing process rubrics is to define more carefully the process to be rated, then to use brief descriptions of the levels to which the student response meets the ideal. This system is very useful in communicating to students the type of reasoning that is expected. It is often difficult to describe a process to students. The rubric gives a way to do this, especially if the students can be involved in helping to define the characteristics of different types of mathematical thinking. Exhibit 10.2, adapted from the Vermont Mathematics Portfolio Assessment Program (Vermont State Board of Education, 1990), gives some good descriptions of mathematical processes that might be starting points for use in classrooms. This rubric is based on problem solving, so the work is rated on four major components of this process. In addition, the rubric rates the students' abilities on two communication processes used to represent and explain the problem-solving approaches and the solution.

Exhibit 10.2. Rubric from the Vermont Mathematics Portfolio Assessment Program.

Problem Solving

Understanding the Task. Understanding can include appreciating relevant information, being able to interpret the problem, and asking key questions that push for clarification. At the lowest level, the student is not able to understand what is being asked. A blank response or clear misinterpretation is indicative of misunderstanding. The highest level of this scale suggests that the student stopped and analyzed the problem statement at the beginning, looked for special cases and missing information, and so forth.

1 point — Totally misunderstood
2 points — Partially understood
3 points — Understood
4 points — Generalized, applied, or extended

Approaches/Procedures/Strategies. Many different strategies should be valued but those that lead to an answer in an appropriate manner are a goal. At the first level, an approach or procedure is chosen that would not lead to a solution. A second-level approach or procedure is workable for some part of the task. If the approach is viable and can lead to a solution, the rating is three. The top level is for approaches that are sophisticated and show particular strengths and efficiencies.

1 point — Inappropriate or unworkable approach or procedure
2 points — Appropriate approach/procedure some of the time
3 points — Workable approach
4 points — Efficient or sophisticated approach or procedure

Choices Along the Way. Good problem solvers use metacognitive actions like checking their assumptions, reflecting on their decisions, analyzing the effectiveness of strategies, checking for exceptions, and verifying results in other ways. At the bottom of the scale is a student who attempts the problem without any evidence of informed decision making. When an inference can be made with some certainty that decision making occurred at some level, then the rating is a three. If decision making may, or just as likely may not, have occurred, then the response is a two. The high end of the scale is a response that clearly articulates the decisions made, either through explanation or example.

Exhibit 10.2. Rubric from the Vermont Mathematics Portfolio Assessment Program, Cont'd.

1 point—No evidence of reasoned decision making
2 points—Reasoned decision making possible
3 points—Reasoned decision making/adjustments inferred with certainty
4 points—Reasoned decision making/adjustments shown, explicated

Findings, Conclusions, Observations, Connections, and Generalizations. A primary objective of problem solving is to make connections to other concepts, extend the solution to other problems, and make observations about conclusions. A level-one response requires a solution, but the student solves the problem and stops. Any attempt to question what the solution means or to make an observation about it leads to a rating of two. If the student goes beyond a simple observation and makes connections to other mathematics, to other disciplines, or to other possible applications, then the rating is a three. When a student synthesizes information or comes to some generalization or level of abstraction based on the observations made throughout the problem, the rating is a four.

1 point—Solutions without extensions
2 points—Solutions with observations
3 points—Solutions with connections or applications
4 points—Solutions with synthesis, generalization, or abstraction

Communication

Mathematical Representation. Communication in mathematics includes being able to represent information through graphs, charts, tables, diagrams, models, and other sorts of visual presentation. In addition, equations, formulas, and other symbolic representations must be used and linked to verbal and visual approaches. At the first level, students make no attempt to integrate representations into their problems. At the next level, representations are used, although they may not be accurate. Level-three responses include accurate and appropriate representations of different types. A level-four rating reflects sophisticated use of representation, of the best methods for communicating ideas in simple but elegant ways.

1 point—No use of mathematical representations
2 points—Some use of mathematical representations
3 points—Accurate and appropriate use of mathematical representations
4 points—Perceptive use of mathematical representations

Clarity of Presentation. Students working with mathematics must be able to organize their thoughts and presentations coherently and with sufficient detail so that another person can understand their line of thinking. Level one is for work that cannot be followed at all. If there are some clear parts but many missing or confusing steps, the rating is a two. A level-three response provides most of the information clearly with only occasional inference needed by the reader. The fourth level is a structured response with detail and clarity throughout.

1 point—Unclear and disorganized, lacking detail
2 points—Some clear parts
3 points—Mostly clear and organized
4 points—Clear, well-organized, and complete

Source: Adapted from Vermont State Board of Education (1990).

This is a very complete rubric that teachers may wish to use only on a weekly problem, important projects, or major assignments. Of course, parts of it may be used on a more frequent basis, especially if there is a focus on a problem-solving process. For example, the teacher may choose to emphasize the process of decision making during problem solving, encouraging students to think about their thinking and communicate how they make choices. The choices-along-the-way rubric could be used to rate students' papers in order to provide feedback and to emphasize the importance of this process.

Exhibit 10.3. Tsuruda Problem-Solving Rubric.

Process
0 points—Unclear method or method that would not lead to a correct solution
1 point—Method that could lead to a correct solution but that contains flaws or false assumptions
2 points—Clear, thoughtful method that could lead to a correct solution

Presentation
0 points—Unclear, incomplete, sloppy description of problem, procedure, and conclusion
1 point—Clear description in some areas but not others; sloppy or careless presentation of solution
2 points—Easily understood, well-organized description of problem, procedure, and conclusion

Answer
0 points—Incorrect/incomplete answer
½ point—Correct answer

Maximum score is 4½ with a correct solution and 4 with an incorrect solution.

A final example of process rubrics (Exhibit 10.3) illustrates the extent to which process and presentation can be emphasized over the correct answer in a problem. This rubric was developed by Gary Tsuruda, a mathematics teacher in Palo Alto, California. He uses the rubric to rate his students' work on a problem-of-the-week assignment. The students receive a process and a presentation score, along with half a point for the correct answer. Some teachers prefer to reserve zero points for a blank paper and to give students at least one point for an attempt. Tsuruda requires that students have a method that could actually work in order to earn one point. Notice that the correct answer is a bonus; students receive full credit if their process is clear and appropriate and the presentation is understandable and organized.

These examples of process rubrics give a wide range of choices and illustrations that can be used or adapted to a particular grade level or situation. For classroom use, it is clear that two of the most important aspects of a rubric are (1) the ideas conveyed to the students about mathematical thinking and (2) the information that the teacher is able to glean on the students' use and development of these processes.

Analytic Rubrics

Another type of rubric is even more focused, designed to score steps or important concepts in a specific mathematical task (Exhibit 10.4). This type of rubric is sometimes called an analytic rubric. The score for a step in a task can be given as an accumulation of points and can be scaled for quality of the response. Consider the following task and accompanying rubric as an example:

Exhibit 10.4. An Analytic Rubric.

The origin O and the point A represent opposite vertices of a rectangle whose area is 24 square inches.

a. What is one possible set of coordinates for point A?
   1 point for a correct pair of coordinates.
b. Mark and label the coordinates of two more points so that the area of the rectangle would be 24 square inches.
   1 point for each correct pair of coordinates.
c. Explain why you chose those two coordinates.
   1 point for saying the product is 24.
   2 points for saying any such points must have a product of 24.
   3 points for expressing a relationship to $A = lw$.
d. Describe the shape of the curve that is formed by connecting all of the points that make a rectangle with an area of 24 square inches.
   1 point for a curve.
   2 points for a curve that approaches the axes.
   3 points for a hyperbola.

An analytic rubric must be constructed for each task and must be able to reflect the types of answers that students might give. The primary purpose of such a rubric is to provide very focused information on mathematical knowledge and processes and to ensure uniformity and reliability in scoring. This type of rubric is very similar to what many teachers use in giving partial credit on assignments and tests. The advantage in its scoring precision must be weighed with the possible disadvantage in the time required to develop the rubric and to score each task. The rubric may not provide valuable feedback to the teacher and student about thinking and problem-solving processes but would furnish specific feedback about particular concepts or procedural steps. Finally, this kind of rubric could be very useful in large-scale assessments in which only brief training is available for raters. The specific directions for assigning points make it possible to achieve high agreement among raters.

Developing a Rubric

We have already suggested that in developing or adapting a rubric teachers must decide whether specific processes are to be assessed or whether a more general rubric should be used. Other decisions include which point scale or scales are to be used and whether the scale should be broken into subscales for individual processes. It also may be important to write out the meaning or descriptors of the scale values and to discuss these with students.

In large-scale assessments, a great deal of time is spent developing and calibrating rubrics so that a high degree of interrater reliability is reached. Raters may actually perform the tasks themselves or spend time discussing a set of student papers before beginning to develop the rubric. Once the raters are highly familiar with the tasks to be scored, they begin to write descriptions of different levels of performance seen in the students' work.

Through a process of discussion and consensus building, the criteria for each level of the rubric are developed. After the rubric is in final draft form, a set of papers is scored. A sample of the papers is scored independently by two or more raters, and their ratings are compared. A simple percentage agreement is usually sufficient to estimate agreement among raters. Often, agreement within one point between raters is used rather than exact agreement. If the percentage agreement within one point reaches 60 to 90 percent, the rubric is judged to be sufficiently clear for reliable distinctions to be made among the levels. If agreements are too low, the criteria are clarified. The midrange scores (three or four on a six-point scale, for example) usually pose the greatest difficulties for rater agreement. Raters are more likely to agree on the low and high papers.

Although the concern about interrater reliability may not be so critical for an individual teacher, it is probably a good idea to use a set of student papers and to develop or adapt a rubric, rather than doing the development completely ahead of time. If colleagues are available, it can also be very helpful to involve them in describing and developing the rubric criteria. Even if a teacher starts with a "readymade" rubric in which minor adaptations are made, the input from others will be valuable. For schools or districts that wish to develop alternative assessment and rubrics for a particular subject or final evaluation, or even for two or three teachers who want to work together on developing a rubric, the approach used by large-scale assessments is worthwhile.

Once the rubric is developed, it may be a good idea to try it out on one or more sets of papers before finalizing it. Many teachers try the scoring system a few times, handing the papers back to students and getting their input, before making it count for a grade. When developing a rubric or beginning to assign scores to papers, Stenmark (1989) suggests that papers first be sorted into general groups according to the major components of the rubric, then divided into other levels. For example, if a teacher is using a four-point rubric, the papers could be sorted into two groups, "high" and "low." Next, each group can be sorted again. Finally, the responses are read again and compared to the descriptions of the corresponding level or score on the rubric. This process can help develop an idea of the criteria or descriptions of the requirements for varying degrees of success. This approach ensures that the rubric accommodates a range of responses that are encountered during investigative or problem-solving work. There are key questions to consider when designing a rubric. Did the student generalize the situation? Has she or he extended the problem? Do I see original thought? Are the conclusions appropriate for the situation? Has the student put together a presentation that is well thought out? Holistic scoring can make a distinction between those students who just memorize facts, rules, and procedures and those who use thinking skills to solve problems.

Teachers are sometimes surprised at the wide variability in student responses to open-ended or nonroutine problems and practical tasks. General holistic scoring is flexible enough to be employed for assessing journals, port-folios, performance items, and other student mathematical products, as well as open-ended questions. For more information, especially on problem-solving and thinking processes, a process rubric can be used. This type of rubric is also very flexible and can be applied to many kinds of student work. Anaholistic rubrics offer the possibility of scoring on several different aspects of the work — from skills, to mathematical understanding, to reasoning pro-cesses. The scores can be added to give a summative score, which is usually more consistent and reliable than a single score on a general scale. The in-dividual anaholistic scores are useful for keeping a profile of student devel-opment on each of two or more areas of mathematical learning. Finally, the analytic rubrics offer the option of specific fine-tuned assessment of skills, concepts, or problem-solving procedures. This type of rubric can be helpful during the learning process for evaluating whether key concepts and skills are learned.

A complete assessment program should probably include the use of more than one type of rubric. Even though a very general one might be adaptable to nearly every situation, there is often a need for more specific information so that both the teacher and the student can assess progress and learning outcomes. The ideal rubric is both time-efficient and capable of providing specific and useful information.

Assigning Grades

The traditional grading system tends to sort individuals based on perceived ability; it uses a narrow focus on right or wrong answers. The bell curve seems to be inherent as a sorting mechanism, whether it is explicit or not. Many teachers assume there are only a certain number or proportion of A's or B's that can be expected. Adjusting scores to the bell curve dooms some students to failure and the vast majority to mediocrity. The advantage of holistic scoring is that grades can be based on the students' total ability, con-tent knowledge, and process ability rather than just on the percentage of correct answers. Many mathematics educators believe that traditional grading of students has had harmful effects. Low grades obviously discourage indi-viduals from mathematics, and high-achieving students often study for high grades rather than with an interest in learning. Learning is a lifelong ac-tivity; it is important that children see it as something that will continue to enrich them as adults. Tests and grades, more than anything else, are probably the main factors that alienate students from further mathematics learning.

An important idea in using process scores is to maintain separate scores rather than to sum them immediately. Both students and teachers often feel more comfortable with a percentage or letter grade. It is very difficult for them, especially in the upper grades where habits are fixed, to think in terms of rubric criteria rather than percentages. In a preparation course for math-

ematics teachers, I recently gave an excellent class member a four rating
out of a possible five on an assignment. Here are the descriptions of the four-
and five-point levels for the rubric I was using and had shared with the class
before the assignment was given:

> Exemplary (5 points) — Completes task with a clear, coherent,
> unambiguous, and elegant explanation; communicates effec-
> tively, shows excellent understanding of the mathematical and
> instructional ideas and processes; identifies all important ele-
> ments, and may include examples and counter examples; ex-
> hibits creativity and excellent design

> Competent (4 points) — Completes task with mostly clear expla-
> nations and examples; includes appropriate resources and com-
> municates effectively; shows understanding of mathematical and
> instructional ideas and processes; identifies the most important
> elements; shows solid planning and organization

The student complained that her completed assignment was better than
an 80 percent or B paper. I agreed with her but pointed out that it was not
a B; it was a four, which indicated effective communication, understanding, and solid planning and organization. However, I thought her assignment could have been more clear and more creative in the use of examples
and ideas. Although the student still was not completely happy, she accepted
this explanation. Her next assignment was a true five. It was much better
than the previous one, was more creative, and showed deeper thought and
understanding. The student did earn an A in the course.

In assigning grades, it is important that teachers use the rubric not
only to score the paper but also to communicate to the students what the
score means and how they can improve their performance. Converting a
four out of five to 80 percent or a three out of four to a grade of C can de-
stroy the entire purpose of alternative assessment and the use of scoring
rubrics. This practice turns the attention to the grade rather than to the standards or criteria set out in the rubric for student performance. A percentage
or letter grade on each individual paper encourages the student to focus
on the bottom line rather than on the processes and skills that need to
be developed. Scores such as understanding — four, solution — four, and
explanation — two, provide much richer information than a single score or
grade of ten out of twelve, 83 percent, or B. The separate process scores
encourage students to see, for example, that they must focus on doing a better
job of explaining their answer on the next task.

Over time, the separate process scores can be monitored and a clear
picture of students' progress in specific areas of mathematical thinking created.
These profiles can also be very useful to the teacher in deciding which students need further work on particular processes or which areas are being

developed better or less well by a certain teaching activity. Teachers who persist and continue focusing on student processes find that students gradually accept and value this type of feedback on their work.

One of the main barriers to implementing alternative scoring systems is concern about using them for "real" tests. Often, teachers utilize process scores to grade homework, projects, group assignments, or even quizzes but are reluctant to use alternative items or scoring for summative tests. It is a good idea to try these approaches on student work that is less "important" or to make trial runs before actually counting them for a grade. But unless alternative scoring methods are used on higher-stakes tests, students will very quickly realize that the traditional test items, rather than performance or problem solving, remain the most valued assessments. If a change is to be made in student attitudes and beliefs about what is important in mathematics learning, performance and problem solving must count on real tests and real grades.

Part Three

CLASSROOM ASSESSMENT MODELS

In this final section of the book, Chapters Eleven to Thirteen present summaries written by sixteen of the eighteen teachers who participated in a graduate course on mathematics assessment that I conducted at Texas A&M University in 1991–92. Each teacher was involved in a project to learn about new assessment approaches, develop his or her own individual plan, and implement it during the school year. The teachers met twice a month to learn about strategies and to discuss their progress with each other. Their classes were videotaped several times during the year; they were given feedback about their teaching strategies; and their students were asked to complete questionnaires about their attitudes and about the types of activities they did in math class. Chapter Fourteen discusses the formal results of the alternative assessments they tried on both the teachers and their students.

Helping Teachers Use Alternative Assessments

We carried out three coordinated components to help teachers plan and implement alternative assessment approaches: information and activities concerning alternative mathematics evaluation designed to build knowledge about new assessment approaches and support implementation efforts; support and feedback for teachers as they developed plans and strategies for student assessment; and development of assessment tasks and materials to support implementation efforts.

Selection of participants. We tried to obtain a diverse group of teachers who worked in rural, suburban, and urban areas; who taught students of different backgrounds and ethnicities; and who had a wide range of abilities and experiences as teachers. The eighteen selected taught from fourth to tenth grades in east-central Texas school districts. The teachers were a very mixed and able group who had been in the field from three to twenty years. All of them had some graduate work (seven of them had completed master's degrees). There were seventeen women and one man. Four were African-Americans, and the rest were white.

Learning about alternative assessment. The course met twice a month through-out the school year. The content of the course was very much like that of Chapters One through Ten of this book. The course provided concepts, information, and strategies for designing multiple approaches to measuring mathematics performance, with special emphasis on helping teachers develop comprehensive assessment plans and furnishing support for classroom implementation. We gave special attention to the assessment models and approaches that have been developed in states such as California, Connecticut, and Vermont. These models offered some good specific ideas about strategies, sample assessment tasks, and approaches to developing scoring rubrics.

Assessment Plans and Implementation

Each teacher developed an initial plan for implementing alternative assessment in one of their mathematics classes or courses. As the year progressed, the plans were adapted or modified. The teachers adjusted their plans as they learned more about alternative assessment and also as they learned more about the reactions of their students. Several of the teachers included their students as active participants in planning the new approaches and putting them into practice.

Except for elementary teachers, of course, the type of class that the teachers selected for trying out these new ideas varied a great deal. The junior and senior high school teachers chose the class they felt most comfortable working with, one in which they thought the content was most compatible with alternative assessment, or one in which they felt students had the greatest need for change or motivation. There was a wide range of reasons for making these selections, and the teachers were not directed to make any particular choice. Complete descriptions of the plans and the way they worked, written by the teachers themselves, are given in Part Three.

Early on, there was a great deal of discussion about what types of assessment changes to make and when. The teachers were encouraged to make gradual modifications and to involve their students, and possibly parents, in plans or discussions of how changes would be made. Teachers were also encouraged to work toward using alternative assessment for a majority of testing and evaluation in the selected class by the end of the year.

During the course, the teachers put their assessment plans into practice and shared experiences about what was effective in their classes. Much of the discussion at class meetings was devoted not only to providing information on assessment but also to fostering the sharing and clarification of approaches that teachers were trying in their classes. The issues that arose consistently often involved

- Approaches to assigning grades
- The use of scoring protocols on open-ended items and problems
- Integration of writing, such as journals, into the evaluation process
- The use of timed tests

- The assessment of group versus individual work during cooperative learning activities
- The attitudes of students in accepting new assessment approaches

As classroom implementation took place, it became clear that much of the discussion about procedures and strategies focused on teaching as much as on evaluation. Many of the teachers' plans for implementing alternative assessment methods were closely tied to strategies for using problem solving or communication activities as a regular part of instruction. For example, several teachers implemented a problem-of-the-week or problem-of-the-day approach to help students develop higher-order thinking abilities. Some of these teachers used the problems as cooperative group activities; others asked students to select their best problem for presentation or evaluation; still others asked students to choose a problem to include in a portfolio.

Several teachers tried group and project assignments, working with hands-on materials or calculators. Although many of the participants were already comfortable with these kinds of strategies, the project and the input from fellow participants encouraged the remaining teachers to try these methods either for the first time or to make them a regular part of their instruction. There were many significant changes in the teachers and their students during the year. Most of the teachers changed their strategies both in assessment and in the way they taught mathematics. They began to emphasize understanding of concepts, focused more on problem-solving strategies, and used more group work and independent projects to give their students more opportunities to be involved. It was clear that when these teachers began to change the way they assessed students, they also changed their teaching to include a wider variety of approaches.

Assessment Models

The teacher summaries in this chapter are offered as models, not because they are perfect, but because they provide ideas and frameworks that can be adapted and modified. Not everything these teachers tried in assessment worked. Their summaries are open and frank, providing insight into the difficulties as well as the successes. Overall, it is clear that the summaries reflect the results from the data collected. More importantly, these stories provide the best kind of information possible to other teachers who are interested in implementing alternative assessment in their mathematics classes. There is enough variety in the types of classes and the goals for evaluation that nearly anyone can find a situation similar to his or her own class. It is always a good idea to learn from others' experiences. The discussions of these teachers during their work were invaluable as a source of support and encouragement. Their experiences can supply similar inspiration to others. Their work provides realistic examples of what it is possible for an individual teacher to accomplish with the information available in this book and the motivation to try something new.

11

MODELS FOR
ELEMENTARY GRADES

IN THIS CHAPTER, WE PRESENT DETAILED SUMMARIES OF ASSESSMENT PROGRAMS written by elementary teachers. The teachers and students represent a wide range of locations, types of schools, and ability levels. Each teacher had specific objectives for implementing alternative assessment, and each worked within varying constraints and availability of support and resources.

The introduction and use of any new approach to teaching or assessment involve extra work and require adjustments on the part of all teachers and students at all levels. However, the elementary teachers in our project had a relatively easier time making these changes than did those in the later grades. For one thing, elementary classes tend to be more flexible and the transitions and distinctions between subjects less rigid. Mathematics can be integrated with other subjects, making it possible, for example, to have students write about mathematics problems as a part of language arts or do an interdisciplinary project that involves reasoning and problem solving. Students in the elementary grades also are more willing to try new ideas. Their notions about the nature of mathematics work and approaches for evaluating their performance are more open to change.

Open-Ended Problems in a
High-Ability Fourth-Grade Class
Ernestine Betchan
Rockdale Elementary School

Rockdale is a small rural community with a population of about six thousand. The town has several independently owned businesses, the largest being the Alcoa Aluminum Plant. A number of residents commute to Austin, Bryan, and other cities. There is a high percentage of college graduates in Rockdale, primarily Alcoa engineers and technicians, as well as plant management personnel.

Rockdale Elementary School has approximately nine hundred students, prekindergarten through fifth grade. As elsewhere, Rockdale has its share of single parent–provider families. Currently, whites are in the majority, with an ever-increasing African-American and Hispanic population. Our school has an extremely high ratio of free- or reduced-lunch students. My fourth-grade math class is made up of twenty-two students who scored very well on achievement tests, were noted by their third-grade teachers to be very good math students, or consistently made high nineties on their math report last year. The fourth grade as a whole is heavily loaded with boys. In my accelerated math class, there are sixteen boys and six girls; two students are African-American, the rest white. Eleven of the twenty-two are in our gifted and talented program, which is a once-a-week, all-day pull-out program.

The students feel competent in solving math problems, and most certainly have a positive attitude toward the subject. Many of my students are involved in community sports, such as baseball, soccer, basketball, or football. They are members of 4H as well as scout troops. Many are actively involved in their respective church choirs; many take piano or dance lessons. There is generally a high parental interest in this group of students. During open house, for instance, my class is full of interested parents. My students are motivated because of parents, but more than that, the majority want to do well for themselves. Each has set a personal high standard of achievement.

We work daily in cooperative groups, individually, or in pairs. I teach the class in a variety of ways. In teaching a new skill, I go over the concept in discussion with the class and do some samples on the overhead. Then we practice a few examples independently or in a group and check for understanding, tutoring anyone who does not understand. The students are very good at peer tutoring, even coming in at break or special program times to help someone. We use many manipulatives in our class. Earlier in the year, as in the past, I gave an end-of-the-chapter test directly from the math textbook. Usually though, I shorten these tests to ten or so problems. Since the beginning of 1992, however, I have tried to look for other ways to give "tests." I rarely assign homework.

Assessment Plan

Initially, my goals for this project were to have the class become better problem solvers, develop portfolios, and change their attitudes toward math problem solving. Strategies I planned to use included open-ended problems on tests or daily assignments, student-generated problems, projects, and assignments to place in portfolios. We also planned to write regularly in a math journal. These as well as other means of assessment would be used to check student progress and confer with parents. When to implement all of this was unclear.

Reports, discussions, and ideas from others, plus their support and encouragement, helped me start with at least part of my plan. We started by copying a problem of the day from the board several times a week. The students loved solving the problems but hated copying from the board. One of the teachers in my group at Texas A&M gave me a copy of a book containing difficult, thinking-type problems. I made copies of a different page every week and allowed the student groups to work together to solve the problems at the beginning of each class time. They would then submit in writing the solution or methods used by their groups. A few people abused the group time at first by not working as hard as the others. I then had the groups "grade" themselves using process-based scoring sheets. This approach, plus the journal entry, seemed to pull in those "lazy" group members.

One of the things they graded themselves on was their written explanation. This was the hardest aspect of all. To get everything written on paper and not to assume anything at all was for a long time very difficult. I also have at least two extremely competitive students who at first did not want to share any information at all.

We often read group or individual explanations out loud. Our plan for these entries has been to check the progress of students; they then can look back and realize how much their writing has improved, as has their group's ability to work together. Each student has turned in several group and/or individual assignments for process-based scoring. These have been used as daily grades as well as test scores.

Though it is still difficult to assign grades to these problems, it is getting easier as time passes. The students understand the process-based scoring and think that it is fair and gives a clear picture of what they know. As we finished geometry this year, we constructed angles and proved degrees in triangles and quadrilaterals by tearing off the vertices. These explanations and products served as our test for this unit of study.

I have found that I am thinking more and solving problems better myself since our participation in this project began. I look for more ways to use manipulatives and open-ended problems. I can look at a finished or partially finished product and tell whether a student understands a skill or concept. I have not carried through with the portfolio idea this year.

The kids have taken a test of different areas of growth in our gifted and talented program and have excitedly reported to me that they all advanced a great deal in the thinking and solving portion of the test. They felt this achievement was due to the project. I think some who were a bit cautious about speaking out in class or sharing ideas have grown because of the written explanations and work within the groups. With these types of problems, there wasn't just one answer or one way to solve them.

There are many days my students ask if they have to go back to homeroom, or couldn't they just stay in math for the day? Outside, my homeroom class hears the excitement within the room or comes in as students are finishing some part of an assignment. They often comment, "Gosh, Mrs. Betchan, I wish I were in your math group! You have fun in here."

Teacher-Constructed Alternative Tests in Fourth Grade
Vyckye Cox
Mission Glen Elementary

The community that feeds into Mission Glen Elementary is largely a still-growing suburb. Just across the street from the school, new homes are being built, and the land adjacent to the playground has recently been cleared for construction. This is basically a working-class neighborhood. Many of the families are two-parent working families; however, the mothers who stay home provide a large volunteer pool for the school. The socioeconomic status of the students varies from students who receive free lunches and live in homes with dirt floors to students who live in $100,000 homes. The ethnic groups composing the community are Hispanic, African-American, Asian, and Anglo. During multicultural week, many parents come to the school to share traditions, customs, and other aspects of their cultures with students and teachers.

Mission Glen Elementary is a kindergarten through grade-five school with approximately 750 students. The school's floor plan is open; the classrooms do not have doors, and the outside wall facing the hallway is only a partial wall that does not meet the ceiling. At Mission Glen, teachers cover blocks of subjects. My block is math, science, social studies, and health. Math is taught first in the morning; however, if a meaningful discussion is going on, the time is often extended. Wednesday is computer day, and the students are taken to the computer lab for forty minutes before returning to the classroom for math. The computer time is usually a problem-solving time where students use Logowriter.

There are twenty students in my class, ten boys and ten girls. There are seven Hispanics, one African, three African-Americans, two Asians, and seven whites. Some students go to the Chapter I classroom for reading, one student goes to bilingual class, and one student goes to a resource classroom for extra help in math and reading. My students have a wide range of interests and participate in sports, dances, and church activities. Most of them seem quite motivated to learn. However, there are a few in the classroom who require a very high level of intensity to attract and maintain their interest in the lesson of the day. Some of the students lack adequate social skills and tend to resolve their conflicts in an aggressive manner.

The class organization is somewhat eclectic. There are times when I lecture. There are times when I help students discover rules, patterns, and so forth through group discussion. I encourage students to discuss and collaborate with one another on word problems and other independent practice activities. I give many tasks in class for which students have to work together to solve the problem. I rely on questioning to get them to think through a problem or to understand a process. Peer teaching has sometimes helped students to grasp a concept.

Students often use manipulatives to keep them actively involved and interested. Much to the surprise of many students, I allow them to use calculators to solve some computations and to do some problem solving. My goal has been to get students "hooked" on math and to enjoy it. At the beginning of the year, students were not very comfortable with this format and were reticent when asked questions. It took them quite a while, but they have finally become used to this practice in the classroom.

School policy requires a routine in math each day that includes a word problem, a review, and a drill and the assignment of ten homework problems per night Monday through Friday. However, I also give other assignments, which students have one week to complete. They can work with someone else and are encouraged to share and discuss the problem with parents or older siblings. These assignments are given every other marking period (we use a six-week marking period) and are used to assess knowledge, to acquaint students with the use of math in everyday life, and to extend their communication of math outside the classroom. Journal articles have been assigned periodically so that students could think about how the math they have been studying relates to everyday lives.

This year, the school began a Family Math Night to encourage families to work with their children on math concepts. The nights have focused on how parents can communicate with their children about math and the things parents can do to reinforce the skills being taught in the classroom. Another commitment of our school is the new technology project that will be implemented in the fourth and third grades. Teachers will have a computer on their desks, and there will be computers—one for each three students—in each third- and fourth-grade classroom.

Assessment Plan

My assessment plan focused on students' knowledge of concepts, ability to solve problems, use of models and symbols in solving and explaining various problems, and ability to use mathematical language to communicate ideas. The assessment plan was implemented with the first test. With a few modifications, the strategies set forth in the initial plan were put into practice. The use of holistic grading was extended to all graded activities, not just process-based ones. Open-ended tests were given, as well as creative testing (such as asking students to justify their answers on multiple-choice items). Students were given problem-solving activities and asked to explain how they solved problems in informal (never formal) assessment and teaching situations.

For decimals, we used manipulatives and various models to evaluate concepts via demonstration. Students had to model tenths, hundredths, and addition and subtraction using the base-ten blocks. During this assessment, some students were interviewed on an individual basis, but this process took too long to allow all students to have an interview. Thus, as a formal assessment, the remainder of the students were observed demonstrating the processes. Manipulatives were also used to gauge students' knowledge of perimeter and area.

Students seem to have become more comfortable with math and with testing. They appear to view testing as a natural extension of math, not necessarily as a separate entity that causes much anxiety. In their journals, they write how math is fun or how some concepts are easy. Students who complained about math at the beginning of the year seemed to become less agitated as the year progressed. Most of the students will participate in math even if they do not take an active role in other activities. There are a few students who still think that math is hard and feel somewhat uncomfortable. However, even they have relaxed to some degree because they have fewer pencil-and-paper tasks.

Through interviews or demonstrations, the Chapter I bilingual student appears better able to show what he has learned. His improved performance on these particular tasks may be due to not having to read and process the meaning of the words. Another student, a constant procrastinator, did better on demonstrations and in the interview because he could not put down just any answer in a one-to-one situation as he often did when given a pencil-and-paper test.

This method of assessment was very time-consuming, both in constructing the test and in grading. I could not just make up a key and begin to grade and record. It took time to read the responses, categorize them, and then assign some value to them. Explaining the scoring system, the purpose of projects and investigations, and the relative lack of graded papers and worksheets to parents was another difficulty.

In spite of the difficulties, some rewards came from the use of alternative assessment. Instead of introducing the rules this year, I have tried to come up with ways that students can create them themselves. This year, I have also made a concerted effort to be more interdisciplinary. I have attempted to tie math into science and social studies and to make students aware that math situations occur not just during math time but throughout the day.

This project has also caused me to think of ways to align my testing with the way I teach. In the past, although I taught using manipulatives, open-ended questions, and group discussions, I had a tendency to use the test provided by the text and just add an essay question or two. However, this year I have made up all of my tests. I have been testing the way I teach. Yet there are times when I feel that the test is too lengthy or that the items are too difficult. There is constant evaluation of what has been done in the hope that next year it will be even more refined.

Testing in this manner, student grades have remained stable or improved. The students who have been the best continue to remain on top. However, some students have said they are doing better this year in math than last year even though they feel the content is more difficult. The students who have had more difficulty are still struggling, but they are at least trying. A few of the students with a negative attitude about math also seem to be having less difficulty than before. They appear less tense when they do math now. Some who would not venture answers have now opened up and will at least attempt a response.

I feel that during this year I have accomplished the objectives set forth in the preliminary plan. The students are beginning to realize that math is not just finding answers and that it is a process that counts. Students are beginning to appreciate math as a process, and some have a more positive attitude about it. Students appear to be better thinkers, writing about their thoughts after they have been formulated. They seem somewhat better able to relate math to their everyday lives rather than see it as a separate entity.

Problem-Solving Portfolios in Fourth Grade
Deborah Godfrey
Spigner Elementary School

W. D. Spigner Elementary School is located in the quiet, small town of Calvert, Texas, a town of about four thousand people between the cities of Waco and Bryan–College Station. The total enrollment of the campus is 231 students: 163 African-Americans, 27 whites, and 41 Hispanics.

My class of fourth graders had twenty-three students — ten girls and thirteen boys with various interests, abilities, and learning styles. With this diversity of interests in mind, I made student motivation one of my primary aims. Student growth, achievement, and motivation through an abundance of praise and reward were essential targets. I emphasized daily the importance of trying to succeed, and the students possessed an eagerness to try. The math center in the room helped to focus my students' attention and inspire them to do well. The center contained materials such as games, puzzles, and manipulatives that could be used for enrichment by individual students. The center also contained posters and bulletin board problems and activities designed to encourage and motivate the students to excel in math.

Being an effective, interesting, and well-prepared teacher has always played a vital role in my instruction. On a typical day, math class began promptly at 10:00 A.M. First, I introduced the daily objective in the most absorbing and engaging way possible through everyday examples and situations related to the students' lives. Next, I solicited total classroom participation through fun approaches. I referred to this period as our warm-up activity. In other words, there was plenty of teacher-student interaction. Instruction concentrated on the use of various manipulatives and hands-on work to assist students with their problem solving as well as to develop their ability to formulate their own problems and solutions. A problem of the day provided a focus for synthesis at the end of each class period.

Homework assignments were a daily part of our learning process. However, realizing that homework could be done with the assistance of a parent or classmate, I also considered it to be a reinforcer for the skills addressed each passing day. Similarly, diagnostic and prescriptive tests were administered continuously to assess and reassess and to track student progress.

Assessment Plan

In the past, I have had mixed emotions about the available approaches to evaluating my students in mathematics. So I was very excited at the prospect of learning and trying new ideas. My initial plan was to explore several possible assessment techniques. After studying and trying several, I decided to focus on the portfolio. My goal was to implement this method and to share this experience with members of my staff. I shared the excitement of participating in the project with my students, who initially were quite uneasy. For example, one student remarked, "Our school is probably the smallest school in the project, and I don't think we can do well." At this point, I assured him that we could do well if we thought we could. Most of the students were really apprehensive about the role their class would play. However, attitudes soon changed, and they were ready for the challenge.

One rewarding aspect of developing a portfolio was the opportunity it provided them to display only their "best" work. For instance, one student asked, "Does this mean nobody will know that I did not do so well when we first started talking about multiplying larger numbers?" "Yes," I replied. I also reminded them that the portfolio would provide the fifth-grade teacher next year with a greater awareness of their abilities. These factors had a great impact on the quality of work the students produced.

The outcome of our assessment was very exciting. Although it was a slow process, students discovered more than one way to solve some problems. A stimulus arose each time it was discovered that one student could solve a problem using multiplication, while a fellow classmate solved it using addition. In fact, students formulated their own problems and were very successful in solving these. The group and cooperative learning settings really enhanced the students' willingness to participate.

This new adventure resulted in many improved attitudes. The students also began to incorporate many science activities into our everyday math problems. Some groups included health activities in their math problems. Finally, implementation of the alternative mathematics assessment was indeed a new and fascinating expedition. I saw my students blossom and take advantage of any and all opportunities to solve problems. Their self-esteem increased. I could see their self-confidence rise as they journeyed up the hill feeling like the little red engine, "I think I can, I think I can, I know I can!"

Assessment Portfolios in the Fourth Grade
Ginny Heilman
Rock Prairie Elementary School

College Station is a small community with a large university. Many of the residents of College Station are connected to the university in some way. There is also oil activity in the vicinity, and a portion of the population fluctuates with the boom and bust of the petroleum industry. College Station is a young community, having recently celebrated its fiftieth year.

Rock Prairie Elementary School is the newest and largest elementary school in College Station. Three years ago, when it first opened, it literally was on the prairie. Now it is totally surrounded by new houses. The school is more than full, and the student population is a mix of extremes: many come from affluent neighborhoods; others are bused from the poorest neighborhoods in town. Of the 735 students, approximately 30 percent represent a minority group.

Each teacher is paired with one other teacher. One teacher handles the language arts–social studies block while the other teaches the math-science-health block. Twenty-two fourth graders were used for this study. The fourth grade uses team teaching. Nine of the twenty-two are girls; one girl is Hispanic, two boys are black, and one boy is Indian. Two of the boys have identified learning disabilities and are resource students on monitored status in math. One boy is currently being evaluated for Attention Deficit Disorder. The majority of the students are strong, average kids with a desire to work hard. There are few discipline problems. This class has an unusually large number of two-parent families who have been exceptionally supportive of me and have high, but reasonable, expectations for their children. Three children joined the class at the beginning of the second semester.

The children in this class generally want to do well. They are able to work well in cooperative groups, a feat that I credit to our third-grade teachers who have stressed collaboration in the last few years. The students respond well to me and show a great deal of respect, which I believe is a reflection of their parents' expectations. The classroom is operated in such a way that the children feel they are actively involved in the whole learning process. They are expected to manage themselves and their work—with help when needed—without my constant interference. One of my goals is to help my students understand that they do have control over their actions, their time (to a degree), and their work. Grouping is done either formally (by assigning a specific role to each student) or informally. The desks are arranged in groups of four or five, so that individuals are often given permission to discuss their work with the people in their group. Weekly seating charts help guarantee that everyone will have a chance to work with all the others in the class at some time.

New concepts are presented at the beginning of the lesson to the whole group using manipulatives, the overhead, or real-world examples, Practice is generally done by each student in a math journal, which I check immediately. I encourage interaction among students as they work the assignments. Any student needing to use manipulatives is encouraged to grab the tool of choice without asking for permission.

Nonroutine problems and other kinds of activities are explored by the children without discussion at first. Then, students come to the board to offer their solutions for the rest of the class to evaluate and discuss. A general atmosphere of "safety" prevails, so no one is afraid to come to the board with a partial solution or an incorrect one. To keep from calling on one or two eager beavers who always want to share their solutions, I draw popsicle sticks. Each student's name is on a popsicle stick in a container. When I need a "volunteer," I draw a stick, and that person is the one who responds. "I didn't get it" is greeted by "Let's work it together" or "Let's see how far you did get." Frequently, I ask students to tell me how they could explain the concept or activity to someone who did not know how to do it to allow them to put their math thinking into words.

Few homework assignments are given. If necessary, I expect students to drill on facts at home or to complete unfinished work from that day's lesson. My feeling is that I would rather be around when they work the assignment so I can monitor them and so they can benefit from the interaction with others. In addition, some parents who value education and good grades tend to check over work and point out the right answer regardless of the student's understanding. This practice colors my views of children's grasp of what they have learned when I evaluate the work.

Daily work is kept until the next class period, where we usually check it together and discuss it before it is collected. Material that we are just learning is graded by using checks. Work that we have practiced is graded with a number grade.

Tests are my least favorite task. Modified book tests are usually used, mainly for convenience. Most tests are a free-response format, as opposed to multiple choice. This year, I included several short answers to the regular test format. In our district, tests and major projects count for 50 percent of the six-week grade.

Assessment Plan

As a workshop leader once said, you need to have some plan in place before you can make changes! It would be satisfying to state that all the portions of the original time line were successfully implemented, but that was not the case. The strategy most completely employed was that of involving the students from the outset. For example, I would say, "This would be a fair test question for students who are expected to understand multiplication." Therefore, we had many opportunities not only to know what would be asked but also to practice giving oral responses in class.

Journals were the most frequently used strategy; most of our student-generated problems were written in them. (Journals have continued to be a source of personal communication between students and me.) This communication was not necessarily verbal. Though journal work was never graded, it was an excellent way for me to measure the level of a student's understanding. In the journal, I could make corrections without the negative feelings attached to work handed in to be graded. The journal was a private place to make an error.

The journals also served to help me gauge the children's understanding in another way. The students created their own word problems and wrote them in their journals. By reading and sharing student-created problems, we could discuss the current concepts in yet another way. Moreover, the journals proved to be a wonderful repository of problem-of-the-day solutions. On Fridays, the students were required to write up the solution for one of the week's problems of the day to be turned in and scored using a process-scoring rubric. There was no risk of losing Monday's solutions by Friday or forgetting exactly what we had done—there was a record of the week's work right there in the journal. To be sure that work was not lost, the journals were not used for any other subject or purpose, and they were kept in the room at all times.

The notion of portfolios was one of the most appealing to me at the onset of this study. It was also one of the least well developed. The children had little notion of what the purpose of a portfolio was and had little experience with filing work in it. It is my opinion that had we begun the year, or even the semester, with the concept of portfolio use firmly in place, we would have had better success. I did save one of their earliest papers from the beginning of the year on rounding off numbers—a task they did miserably on—and gave it to them to put in their portfolios. We discussed how they had grown over the months they had been in school and how a portfolio of their work throughout the year could help them track their progress. The idea of having a sample of their work from each year throughout their school careers appealed to them.

Small-group instruction has continued—not on the daily scheduled basis as first anticipated, but on an as-needed basis. Because everyone at some point participated in the original group, working in small groups with me has lost any negative connotations it might have had if it had been used only for children who were experiencing difficulty. Flexible grouping has allowed children to explain their thinking to me. In some respects, this fulfills part of the goals of student interviews.

The original plan proposed that math projects be assigned at the end of the year. What a mistake! There were far too many interruptions in our planned routines at the end of the year to aim for a major project. Another difficulty has been my personal lack of experience with math projects. I have a list from Dale Seymour Publications listing many potential projects; however, I am not certain which would be appropriate for fourth-grade students. Other teachers have mentioned this same problem when looking for math projects. Certainly, the existence of this plan has at least made me more aware of what evaluation should be. I hope I will be moving toward having this assessment plan each year. Changing attitudes is a big first step, so while I am disappointed in not following my plan to the degree I intended, I am encouraged by my new awareness of alternative assessments.

One unexpected impediment was a new math text. New materials create a strain. Working with our new math text has proved to be a big adjustment for the students and teachers alike. Major concepts are presented quite differently than in the previous text. Learning how to use the format for the new math series was a challenge to the students. We were advised by the publishers to follow the book to help the students work through any problems. The fourth-grade team stuck to the book as much as possible to try bridge the transition. Wading through a new text took time away from implementing new assessment strategies. Our district has no math curriculum document either, a situation further compounding the difficulty.

One of the most successful new assessment measures for us was the problem of the day. Using process-based scoring on this problem was new for both the students and me. They really honed their ability not only to find the correct solution but also to write complete explanations. It was rewarding (and sometimes amazing) to students that they could get credit for their thinking even if the solution was not perfect.

My favorite example was a girl who always did horribly on low-level routine skill practices. Once she had to redo a review of column addition three times in order to get a passing grade. She is not a slow learner; drills are just not interesting for her. When we began doing group solutions for the problems of the day, she really found her chance to shine. While working in a group, she would provide encouragement and positive responses to all her group members. She did not always know how to arrive at the correct solution, but she was the perfect person to keep a group working. Her written explanations were beautiful! Had we not done the problem of the day and process-based scoring, I never would have seen that lovely side to her.

At the conclusion of a unit on measurement, my teaching partners and I set up a lab practical test. There were nine stations set up around the counter in the science lab. At each station, there were task cards with the appropriate tools to carry out the task. This test covered measurement in centimeters, comparing lengths of different objects, reading graduate cylinders, telling time, and reading a thermometer. The test was not a part of the original assessment plan, but the idea developed naturally as a result of readings for this class and the need to evaluate the students' abilities in measurement. We thought setting up stations in the lab would be the ideal situation. It turned out that it took a long time to get six classes of students through the test. Next year, we will set it up in our rooms so students can work through the tasks during free study periods.

The children are proud of the growth they have made this year in math. They do say they worked hard at understanding what they were doing and at helping each other. Much of this progress comes from the attitude we had while working in the journals, working on the problems of the day, and discussing how to explain new concepts in their own words. Their understanding what I expected them to know at the end of a chapter was an important part of their feeling successful. Evaluating students' attitudes is a task that is subject to many outside interferences. Overall, I would say the children gained a more complete understanding of the math concepts by having been given opportunities to share their knowledge in a variety of acceptable ways. They certainly enjoyed experimenting with new methods of doing things.

Mathematics Journals in Fourth Grade
Diane F. Scott
Briargate Elementary School

My school is located in a socially and economically stable community that survived the devastating blow of Texas's severe recession. Most residents are employed, with many even owning and operating their own businesses. A small segment of the population receives some type of government assistance; most of these residents live in a small section of rental units. The community is experiencing some confusion due to the poor statewide assessment scores achieved by many of its students. A stable residential community should produce moderate, if not excellent, students. The "powers that be" seem to attribute the poor scholastic achievement to the students' race or low socioeconomic status, as opposed to the complacency of many residents, administrators, teachers, and students toward a system that is not serving the needs of those children.

The school serves approximately nine hundred students of primarily African-American heritage. The administration and staff are about 50 percent white and 50 percent African-American. There is an early childhood program available for physically handicapped students who are later mainstreamed into the regular education classes. There is one resource–content mastery class for grades kindergarten through five and two Chapter I teachers in grades three through six.

My fourth-grade class is composed of twenty students: nineteen African-Americans and one Hispanic; ten boys and ten girls. They are grouped heterogeneously, ranging in reading levels from above average to as much as three years below. Their math levels, however, seem to offer less of a range, from above average to two years below grade level. This group is probably the most "loving" group of children I have encountered during my teaching career. However, at the beginning, certain social skills that do enable achievement and success were lacking. Verbal responses, written communication, and expression of confidence seemed quite inadequate among most of the students. The first half of the year required adjustments on the part of my students and myself. What I expected from them had not been consistently required of them in the past, at home or at school, and their lack of self-confidence became more of a deterrent than I had anticipated.

I believe that every individual has some distinctive quality to offer. It is my right and responsibility to bring this quality to the surface. The sharing of experiences can and does serve as models that in some way will "touch the soul" and result in the development of an individual. There are many components that assist in this development. I believe our children should be encouraged to maintain their curiosity and enthusiasm to learn. Curricula that mandate thinking skills can help achieve this. Since children learn in different ways, I have found it necessary to offer "whole brain" lessons. These, based on the presentation of concepts via writing, pictures, objects, and the like, allow the students to feel comfortable in bringing their varied degrees of individuality to the classroom and to build confidence as a result.

Cooperative grouping is another method I incorporated in my teaching. It helped to encompass instruction that reaches the three modalities of learning — visual, auditory, and kinesthetic. The use of manipulatives, as well as the need to work together, allowed the students to interact with one another and to observe a continuous learning process, enhanced by each other's individuality. My students were given daily homework assignments to reinforce past and present concepts. Most of the assignments were practical tasks whose purpose was to make the students understand the necessity of learning the skill. The students were assessed on a weekly basis, either using performance or practical tasks. We used manipulatives such as base-ten blocks, Cuisennaire rods, tangram pieces, attribute pieces, play money, geoboards, and MIRAs. Calculators were also used on a regular basis.

Assessment Plan

As mentioned earlier, one of the biggest obstacles I encountered this year was the lack of self-confidence in my students. This was especially true in the area of mathematics. The students were accustomed to the traditional math lessons and assessments. The challenge not only to obtain the correct answer but to illustrate via diagrams, graphs, tables, manipulatives, or oral or written communication was overwhelming.

I therefore decided to have my students set up math journals to use for specific math problems. These varied in their length, the number of steps needed for a solution, and the degree of difficulty. Initially, I presented the students with a very general format in setting up the journal: one, discussion of the problem; two, selection of a strategy; three, the solution; and four, an explanation of the solution(s). The purpose of the journal was to see how and when my students were able to learn a concept and apply it. Since most of the students had never experienced this approach in mathematics, I set a time line of six months. It took approximately three months to implement the second part (selection of a strategy) successfully. The students only seemed secure when I worked through each problem with them. I then decided to allow them to work the problem cooperatively.

Suddenly, discussions seemed endless. Leaders emerged, and the walls of fear began to collapse. A willingness to try, fail, and try again evolved. The discussions led to more and more strategies, which in turn led to more and more solutions, which in turn led to a greater sense of achievement. Once this occurred, I required the students to work independently. The change in their attitude allowed them to realize that the major difficulty stemmed from their own fears.

In addition to the journal form of assessment, I also had the student work on numerous manipulative activities (independently and cooperatively). Not only did they have to perform the required tasks, they were also responsible for submitting a paragraph explaining their rationale for arriving at a particular solution. Other assessments were given via practical tasks (for example, programming the VCR for the library to record *Reading Rainbow* for the primary grades; making their own meter sticks and then using them to measure the lengths of the teachers' cars; determining how much of each ingredient I would need to prepare tacos for the class).

Many of the assessments were graded traditionally. However, I also used a five-point holistic grading scale:

0 points: Unable to even copy the problem down

1 point: Copied the problem but no further work

2 points: Copied the problem and chose an operation to use in the solution; not necessarily the right operation

3 points: Copied the problem, chose the right operation, and started a solution

4 points: Copied the problem, chose the right operation(s), worked the problem, but did not get the correct answer

5 points: Copied the problem, chose the right operation(s), worked the problem, and got the correct answer

As an educator, it is my responsibility to keep abreast of the constant changes that occur in my field so that I may better prepare my students for the challenges they will encounter in their future. It is my duty to be involved with new ideas in the field of mathematics and to make sure these are implemented to the best of my ability. Making sure that the NCTM *Standards* and the essential elements identified by my state are addressed in my lessons and my teaching is essential. Because of the diverse abilities that exist today within our student populations, keeping abreast of the alternative forms of assessment is a must.

12

MODELS FOR
MIDDLE GRADES

THE MIDDLE GRADES ARE CRITICAL YEARS IN MATHEMATICS AS WELL AS OTHER subjects. Students begin to make choices and exhibit preferences that have implications for future course selection and careers. In many schools, the middle-grades curriculum is shifting toward interdisciplinary and team-teaching approaches. These changes make alternative assessment strategies especially relevant. Mathematics can be taught and evaluated in a variety of settings and subject areas. Students in the middle grades are able to participate in a wider range of learning activities and have developed their ability to communicate mathematically. They are making a transition from learning primarily through concrete approaches to the use of symbolic and verbal strategies. These maturing mathematical abilities provide a rich opportunity for the use of multiple assessments.

At the upper-middle grades, however, teachers and students are concerned with making the transition to high school. Some teachers begin to be concerned about "covering the material" and teaching students to learn from the kind of lecture-oriented instruction that is the norm in high school. These issues can create certain constraints, making it necessary to focus on instruction and assessment that not only develop thinking, reasoning, and communication abilities but also pay close attention to the content background as students begin their study of algebra and other advanced courses.

Mathematics Assessment of Talented Fifth Graders
Rebecca Burghardt
Oakwood Middle School

Oakwood Middle School is the fifth- and sixth-grade campus of the College Station Independent School District. This school serves approximately nine hundred students and is located in a university community of 51,000 people. The entire student population of the College Station Independent School District consists of five thousand students, of whom 73 percent are white, 8 percent are Hispanic, 13 percent are African-American, and 6 percent are predominantly Asian. Twenty-one percent of the students are identified as economically disadvantaged, and 3 percent have limited English proficiency.

The class in which I implemented the alternative assessment project contained twenty-three identified gifted and talented students, twelve boys and eleven girls. Four of these were Hispanic, two were Asian, and seventeen were white. As a group, they were highly motivated, with abilities ranging from slightly above to well above average. The range of abilities in this class appeared to stem from the selection process. Oddly enough, one of the criteria for placement in the gifted and talented mathematics program required that the students first qualify for the same program in language arts. From this group, students were chosen for gifted and talented mathematics. I believe that many of our school's highly talented mathematics students were overlooked in this identification process. We have proposed changes in next year's selection methods to consider the entire school population, without regard to identification in another area.

The class was taught using a new curriculum based on the NCTM *Standards*. The curriculum was written last summer as part of a project with Texas A&M University. The curriculum stressed mathematical reasoning, problem solving, communication, and connections. Each six-week unit was organized around a broad theme in which all of the strands of mathematics were taught: problem solving; patterns, relations, and functions; number and numeration concepts; operations and computation; measurement; geometry; and probability, statistics, and graphing.

Classroom organization centered around group work with the teacher's role being to facilitate learning. Topics were generally introduced by the teacher to the whole class at the beginning of each lesson, and then all work was done in cooperative groups. The groups were highly structured; each group member played a vital role in the success of the efforts. Groups of four students rotated through the roles of investigator, manager, organizer, and recorder-reporter. The investigator manipulated the materials and asked questions of the teacher. The organizer gathered and organized the materials and directed the cleanup. The manager helped the investigator, kept time, performed calculations, and encouraged the group. The recorder-reporter wrote down the group's observations, wrote down answers to questions, made drawings as needed, and shared the group's results and conclusions with the class. The roles greatly facilitated the smooth running of cooperative group activities. For example, the role of the investigator reduced the number of raised hands asking questions during activities. Students were encouraged to ask for help from group members first; then, if a question of the teacher was needed, the group formulated it to be asked by the investigator. The role of the organizer ensured that only a few students were moving around the room securing materials. Following group activities, lessons were then usually closed with a whole-class discussion or sharing of each group's findings, solutions, or observations. Short assignments were given daily as homework to allow the students some independent practice or reflection on the topic covered in class. These assignments were often journal-type reactions to the mathematics covered that day.

The implementation of an alternative assessment plan was a goal of mine as a result of my participation in a middle-school mathematics project in the spring of 1991. In this project, teachers of middle-school students were taught teaching strategies that incorporated the NCTM *Standards*. As I took the information back to the classroom and tried the activities with students, I was thrilled to see their increased enthusiasm for mathematics. The students were much more involved in learning and communicating mathematical ideas and in explaining paths to solutions. When the time came for testing, however, I reverted to a more traditional style, using multiple-choice test items or problems that involved a single step and had only one "right" answer. Even though I was teaching in a different way, I was not evaluating students' learning compatibly. During the latter part of the project, I had the opportunity to pilot test a few alternative assessment items. Through the use of open-ended application problems, I gained invaluable information about the mathematical understandings and misconceptions of my students during one of their units of study. It was important to me to begin the year implementing some of the assessment strategies I had learned in an effort to link my instruction and my assessment.

Assessment Plan

The first step was to become familiar with what the NCTM reform leaders and groups like the California Mathematics Council were recommending as ideal assessment. They state that the purpose of assessment should be to improve learning. With these major directives as a guide, I set my own goals for this year: to identify student attitudes toward mathematics, to evaluate group problem solving, to link instruction and assessment through mathematical investigations, to involve students in self-assessment, and to incorporate student portfolios.

Using my experiences from last year, I first initiated alternative assessment of problem solving. Students were given one nonroutine problem each day as a preclass activity. They worked this problem in cooperative groups, justifying their answers to each other. Many students invented their own procedures if the problem involved mathematics for which they did not yet know a formula or algorithm. The drawing of models was encouraged. Then the entire class discussed strategies for finding a solution. By sharing different approaches to working the problem, the students discovered that there were often many ways of thinking about a problem and finding a solution.

As a result of these daily experiences, the students showed increased persistence, flexibility, and confidence in their problem-solving abilities. At the end of the week, they chose one of the daily problems to write up. These written exercises required the students to explain in detail their paths to finding a solution and to discuss why they chose that particular problem to write about. These written items were then graded using a process-based scoring rubric that included an evaluation of the student's grasp of the problem, solution, and explanation. The use of the rubric seemed to communicate to the students the importance I placed on demonstrating an understanding of the problem. I also gained valuable insight into their attitudes toward mathematics by requiring them to discuss why they chose a specific problem to write about. One student wrote, "I chose this problem because I think patterns are fascinating. Also, I enjoy working with pictures." Another showed her pride by saying, "I chose this problem because I figured it out entirely by myself and a boy at my table said it was 12, but I proved that he was wrong. I also like this problem because I like problems like this." The results of these weekly problem-solving papers were averaged together for one of the test grades of the six-week grading period.

I next attempted to assess reactions to mathematics presented in a historical perspective. Every two weeks, I read the students a biography of a famous mathematician from Reimer & Reimer's *Mathematicians Are People Too* (1990). These colorful stories made the mathematicians' lives and work tangible. The students could think about the mathematical concepts discussed and have a real "human" person to hang them on. I then asked the students to write an essay reacting to an individual and/or his or her mathematics. The results were fascinating. After reading about Joseph La Grange, one student wrote the following:

> I think Joseph La Grange was a very bright and smart man. If Joseph hadn't thought of the metric system, I don't think as many people would be involved in mathematics because of the complexity of doing it the other way. Since there is a simple way to measure lengths, we have found out a lot of things we might not have found out doing it another way. From what I've heard about Joseph's teaching method, I admire him and his patience with his students. One thing that amazed me was that Joseph married a woman 20 years younger than him. His wife really supported him in going back into mathematics. That fits the statement, "Behind every good man there is a greater woman."

Another student found Leonard Euler impressive:

> Today, I heard the miraculous story of Euler. This story was
> so interesting because I know about the Euler number. He was
> very fun and neat! Even though I'm a visual learner, I'm sure
> that even an auditory learner wouldn't be able to do headwork
> like Euler used to do. His work was also very amazing. The
> achievements he made were very impressive. My favorite dis-
> covery was the Euler number discovery. I think he deserved
> to have it named after him. His story was my favorite. He
> worked on things I love, like geometry. He seemed to be not
> as strange as other mathematicians. He didn't die very drasti-
> cally like others. Even though he lived a sad life, he was a very
> happy man to me. I hope I will be a wonderful mathematician
> like him when I grow up.

These reaction papers were graded by a check, check plus, or check
minus using effort as a scale. These went into the calculation of a six-week
class participation grade. I did not dare attempt to assign a letter grade to
this type of affective mathematical experience.

My next efforts in alternative assessment stemmed from my desire
to link instruction and assessment through mathematical investigations and
projects. The students were covering a unit in statistics from *Used Numbers*
(Friel, Mokros, & Russell, 1992). The students had learned how to organize
data using line plots and stem and leaf plots. They had also covered measures of central tendency (the mean, median, and mode) and had participated in activities analyzing what the mean tells us and what it does not.
I wanted to gauge the ability of students to organize and analyze data and
wanted them to feel that the learning process was continuing.

From *Used Numbers*, I found an investigation that I used for assessment. Students used data about the grams of sugar per serving in a variety
of breakfast cereals to examine the hypothesis that those with a higher sugar
content are placed on the middle shelf of the grocery store, where young
children are most likely to see and select them. The purpose of this "test"
was to measure the students' understanding of data organization and their
analysis of measures of central tendency. In an effort to make the assessment more meaningful and integral to learning, we began the first day by
weighing common objects with balances and exploring the amount of a gram.
I then passed out cereal boxes and asked students to find the amount of sugar per serving listed in the nutritional information. Students compared the
different cereals and also their sugar content to that of other common foods.
On the second day, students began the actual test. In their cooperative groups,
they completed the data organization, data descriptions, and estimations and
calculations of the mean, median, and mode. This process took the students
three full class periods to complete. The students were then asked to individually write a brief final report comparing the three sets of data, using illustra-

tions. These reports were done as homework over two days; the entire packet was then turned in for grading. Points were awarded for completion of all graphs, estimations, calculations, and descriptions and for the writing of the final report.

What surprised me the most when I examined the students' work was the amount of applied knowledge the students demonstrated. If I had tested them in a traditional way, I am certain that I would never have known that they knew so much! I wondered about the number of times I had given a multiple-choice test and had not allowed my students to show me all of what they knew. How frustrating it must be to know material well and to be asked to bubble in an answer! Another satisfaction of this assessment came from the students' comments about it. Several students openly expressed their appreciation of a test that made them feel they were still learning. Another student wrote to me, "I have thoroughly enjoyed this project and hope you give another one like this some time." One of the eye-openers of the test came from my casual request that students use illustrations in their final reports. My idea was that they could choose some way to summarize their data comparisons graphically. Many students did just that, but some took the word *illustrations* literally and, in their fifth-grade style, created charming cartoons with captions to describe scenarios of cereal buying.

With these implementations of alternative assessment working successfully, I continued with my plan and involved the students in self-assessment. Since most of their work was done in groups, I attempted to evaluate their performance by using a Group-Performance Rating Form from the Connecticut Common Core of Learning Assessment Project, published in *Arithmetic Teacher* (Collison, 1992). On this form, the students were asked to rate themselves on participating in the group, staying on the topic, offering useful ideas, being considerate, involving others, communicating, and contributing to the overall experience. They then circulated their self-ratings to each person in their group for his or her review and signature. If any member of the group disagreed with the rating, the two students could discuss the reasons for the disagreement and decide whether to change the original rating.

After reviewing the completed forms, I was disappointed that I had introduced this process so late in the year. I believe that some of the negative behaviors in groups could have been alleviated had I attempted this approach earlier. The students were extremely honest in their self-evaluations; they pointed out difficulties I had observed and had many times attempted (unsuccessfully) to correct. Problems like dominating the group discussions, getting off the topic, and making inconsiderate comments about a group member were admitted if they had occurred. Students also gave themselves credit for doing a good job in group work. The students recognized their strengths and weaknesses and in later discussions suggested strategies to improve their weak areas. This type of reflective self-evaluation of group interactions seemed to empower the students to improve their cooperative behavior. Once they accepted ownership for a problem, they could deal with it.

My last goal was to initiate student portfolios. In January, students began a file of self-selected work (problem solving, projects, investigations, reaction papers, and so forth). The students were told that from this work they would be allowed to choose four to ten items to be sent to their sixth-grade teacher to illustrate their best work and growth over the year. This has been a very loosely structured venture and has resulted in about 40 percent of the students actively updating and maintaining their files. Next year, I intend to require a more complete sampling of different types of activities as suggested in Stenmark's NCTM publication, *Mathematics Assessment: Myths, Models, Good Questions, and Practical Suggestions* (1992); I will also require that all students compile a complete portfolio with a focus on student thinking, growth over time, mathematical connections, student reactions, and the problem-solving process.

Looking back over the year, I am pleased with the progress I have made toward the implementation of alternative assessment in my classroom. I have a long way to go in fully incorporating an ideal evaluation program, but I am continuing to read and consider new ideas and strategies to improve the evaluation of my students. I now view assessment as embedded in instruction and realize its importance not only in making decisions on the progress of my students but in measuring the effectiveness of my own instruction as well. As Stenmark says, "Students should be working on worthwhile investigations or tasks and their success should be evaluated in ways that make sense" (1989, p. 3).

Comprehensive Assessment in Sixth-Grade Honors Math
Barbara Raines
Lake Travis Middle School

Lake Travis Middle School is located about fifteen miles west of Austin, Texas. The school district has approximately 2,000 students; 450 of those are in middle school. The students are basically middle class, with only 1 percent minority attendance. There is strong support in the community for college preparatory education; therefore, the honors math program has a waiting list of students. In the middle school, there is a sixth-grade honors math program, a seventh-grade honors math program (prealgebra), and an eighth-grade honors math program (algebra I). About 50 percent of the eighth-grade honors math students continue their mathematics education all the way through calculus in high school.

The class observed throughout the semester was the sixth-grade honors math class. It was composed of thirty-one bright and eager students, eleven of them girls. Twelve of the students were in the gifted and talented program in our school. All but three students were also enrolled in the honors language arts program. It was with the assistance of the language arts teacher that I was able to capture extra time for the students to finish their writing projects. One added note of importance: ten of the top students were so highly motivated to learn math that they stayed after school every Monday afternoon for enrichment problems. Starting in October, these students and I worked on various problem-solving exercises, number sense, and algebra. They had so much zest for math that they set wonderful examples for the rest of the students to follow. Out of the entire class, there were very few students who did not do their homework. Only five of the students opted to go into regular math because of scheduling conflicts with sports.

I run my class as a business. Students—as employees of my "corporation"—have individual jobs and job descriptions to fulfill. They each receive a "paycheck" bimonthly (less "taxes") and maintain a "bank account." I direct a tremendous amount of questioning at the students, although some decisions are left to the student who acts as the business manager and her or his assistant. I give lectures on new material and follow up with homework assignments. Some students give lectures to the class. Problem-solving activities are used throughout the entire curriculum. The students also work in collaborating groups on many assignments. I constantly ask the students "why?" and "what if?"

There is an average of three assignments per week, with some assignments on Friday. Most of the other time, we spend in discussion or discovery time. Tests are given about once every six weeks, a reduction from previous years. With alternative assessment, I find that I do not "test" the students as much. There are many more projects, essays, interviews, reflections, and performance-based activities that provide the necessary grade. In closing this section, I do want to state that my students were a joy to teach, and I really appreciate their desire to be the best "guinea pigs" they could!

Assessment

Prior to enrollment in the Alternative Assessment Project at Texas A&M University, I had no knowledge of alternative assessment for mathematics. During the first class, I became aware of the many forms of student evaluation (structured interviews, informal interviews, holistic scoring, analytic scoring, observation, take-home tests, content checklists, assessment through pictures and through manipulatives, self-evaluation, peer evaluation, student portfolios, and student journals), and I was going to try as many as I could! I understood that I was taking on a big job, but I knew I had a lot to learn. I did try many of the new tools throughout the school year and ended it with a large project that included seven of the alternative forms mentioned above. The following discussion will describe the forms I used, the successes and difficulties I encountered, the effects on teaching and learning, and the student reactions.

Structured Interviews

In order to interview each student in a class of thirty-one, I had to give packets of work that took them all week to finish. In some cases, I gave little direction for the work, so that collaboration had to take place in order for each student to finish. The interview was a short session in which students evaluated themselves on their progress in the class. Any difficulties that appeared at this time (semester break) were followed by a parent call. The information I received was a very valuable tool for the parent conferences. The students were impressed that I was personally involved with each of them.

Holistic Scoring

I evaluated my students on a holistic grading scale for two six-week grading periods. I expanded the Vermont Assessment Program to include a five-point scale (instead of four points). The five-point scale was easier to convert to the 100 percent program that I had always used. A perfect paper was given five points. Four points meant an understanding of the work with minor flaws; three points, understanding with a major flaw; two points, partial understanding; one point, no comprehension even though an attempt was made; and zero points, no work at all. Holistic grading was a revelation. The students really began to comprehend the process of understanding. I found that I had to open an afterschool tutorial because students wanted to learn what they missed.

During the fifth grading period, I tried some modifications of the holistic grading scale. I changed to a four-point scale, giving a five — or perfect paper — only on tests or quizzes. This approach lowered the top grading scale, but that effect was what I wanted. For the last grading period of the year, I completely modified the holistic scale to try the point scale I learned at an NCTM presentation by Gary Tsuruda at Jordan Middle School in Palo Alto, California (Tsuruda, 1992). He suggested a two-point scale for the process, a two-point scale for presentation, and a bonus half-point for the correct answer. This would seem to be an easier grading scale because the variation is smaller. For example, zero measures an incorrect process, one denotes a little understanding, and two measures understanding.

Student Self-Evaluation

Self-evaluation was a key factor throughout the holistic grading period, as well as when the students were in groups. When assigning grades for homework, I asked the students to assess their own papers for understanding. When assigning grades for group work, I asked the students to evaluate their partners as well as themselves for cooperation and responsibility (grading on a five-point scale). An evaluation in the form of a reflection was added to every major test. The students were asked to rate their study habits and their preparedness for the test. The reflection was a tremendous tool in assessing the students' difficulties; the information was also helpful for parent conferences.

Student Journals

I tried to use journals throughout the entire school year and found that I still don't know how to be efficient in grading them. Communicating comprehension through writing is so very important, but the awesome job of reading all the journals proved too much. When I reduced the frequency of the journal entries, I found that the journals were not so effective because they were not done every day. Journals were used later in the year for routine situations (basic computation skills) but never with a consistent purpose. I was finally able to use the journals in the large Olympic project at the end of the year. Students were responsible for incorporating their journal entries into the final presentation.

Assessment Through Pictures

I was also able to use both photography and videotaping for assessing the students during the Olympic project. Students were allowed to share their experiences on the videotape in group format and display their work through individual photographs during the Olympic Fair event. Both types of pictures were special to the kids and proved beneficial to me as documentation for next year's project.

Cooperative Learning

Cooperative groups were used all year for problem-solving activities. The students always worked well together (they chose their own groups), finished the work in a timely fashion, and did nearly perfect work. However, with the schoolwide Olympic Fair as the final product, tension and stress arose in the groups. In each student's reflection on the Olympic Fair project, there was a genuine revelation about working together as a team and problem solving under stress. I sometimes suspect that as educators we simulate real-world situations; the students seldom have a chance to face real situations with real stress and complications. The students had to prove to the whole student body and to the administration that they could run an Olympic Fair, from opening ceremony to closing ceremony.

Student Portfolios

Portfolios were another assessment form with which I experimented but still found difficult to master. I attempted "notebooks" but found the grading to be as cumbersome as the journals. I had the opportunity to attend various workshops on portfolios in Washington, D.C., as well as at the NCTM conference in Nashville. Supporters of portfolios in California, Vermont, and Kentucky all suggested that best efforts be chosen for the contents. A California educator proposed a completion grade for portfolios, whereas a Vermont educator suggested combining some student-chosen "best" work with teacher-selected items. The Kentucky educator required a student's reflection every time a paper was chosen for the portfolio. I did discover that one important feature of portfolios was a table of contents. Organization was key to this process.

Final Plan for Alternative Assessment

My original plan was to have many alternative assessment forms within one major project, which eventually became an Olympic Fair. During the course of the planning period, the students were asked to plan one full day of Olympic games that would engage the entire student body. After writing essays about which committee they wanted, the students were divided into five groups: opening ceremony, closing ceremony, public relations, foreign-money exchange, and the Olympic committee. Each committee then elected a leader who was given parameters about the events and was asked to perform certain duties. Journal entries were made every time the committees met. Inside and outside of class, students built booths to display materials from a few predetermined countries; collected food from the PTA to serve at the booths; persuaded the band to play the "Olympic March" for the opening ceremony; had student "ambassadors" give short speeches about some countries; persuaded the librarian to make slides of cultural scenes; set up games and rules for the students to play; and designed medals and a platform for gold, silver, and bronze medalists who won the top three prizes at the games. I don't believe I have ever seen so much decision making and problem solving as on the final day.

As the final assessment for the project, students had to complete a written evaluation. They were asked to write an introduction about the purpose of the project; list three problems that arose and explain how each was solved; provide a photograph; write a reflection on the project and an evaluation of their classmates who served on their committee; include a copy of a product from their committee (program, foreign money, and so forth); and furnish a drawing of a game, its rules, the statistics of the game players, and a graph of the data.

Conclusions

I believe that I have had more growth this year as a teacher because I was involved in this alternative assessment project. I have reevaluated my teaching methods, sought new ways to test learning, become aware of the valuable programs already in use in such states as California and Vermont, and attended five different workshops on assessment throughout the school year. As department chair, I have also changed the entire honors math placement process through the use of nonroutine problems and essays.

Cooperative Problem Solving in Honors Geometry

Scott Samuelson
Lamar School

Bryan and College Station are located in Brazos County in east-central Texas. Bryan has a population of approximately fifty-five thousand, and College Station has about forty-five thousand. There are about ninety manufacturing industries along with Texas A&M University, which has approximately 42,000 students. Each city has its own school district. Bryan Independent School District is the largest employer in Bryan with more than 1,400 employees and 11,500 students. I teach at Lamar, formerly a fifth-grade campus, now a renovated ninth-grade campus. Renovations and lack of supplies continued throughout the first two six-week marking periods. We started the year with about 850 students and currently have 780. The ethnicity is about 30 percent African-American, 26 percent Hispanic, and 44 percent white.

My class is a geometry class of thirty-four ninth-grade honor students. The makeup of the class is fourteen boys and twenty girls. There are two Hispanics, one Asian, and thirty-one whites. Most are at or above grade-level ability. However, only one-third are highly motivated. All of these students are involved in extracurricular events (most in two or more), such as sports, honor society, student council, math and science clubs, foreign language clubs, cheerleading, youth groups, and scouts.

I would describe my teaching as being mostly lecture format with a great deal of questions and answers and with discovery lessons in each chapter. For two years, I was the only teacher for this geometry course at my school. Because Bryan went to a sixth-to-eighth-grade middle-school concept, the two junior highs combined to form a single ninth grade. At Lamar, there are two of us teaching the honors geometry sections. There is some collaboration between us as to presentation of material and test creation, but there is no teaming on lesson plans or teaching. I work primarily with colored chalk on the board. I use the room and a collection of visual aids to demonstrate concepts. Most of the visual aids come from previous students' projects. Many of my examples are drawn from or apply to real-world situations. My style of lecture is upbeat with lots of movement between blackboards, abundant humor, and much interaction between me and my students and between students. My philosophy is that if students cannot have fun learning, it is not their fault.

I have always used a variety of assessments. Most of my quizzes are take-home exams; a few are done in class. However, I do not like using class time for simple regurgitation of book facts. I would rather give problems that integrate concepts. Students need more time to work these types of items. Some students need more time to visualize the solution, and some do not perform well under pressure. For these reasons, I give them the opportunity to take quizzes home where they can use their notes and books and take the time to do the problem(s) well and understand what they are doing.

The students are usually given between four and seven days to complete the exams. The problems require the students to use all their acquired skills, and they must write up each problem, telling what formulas they will use and how, and showing all their work. Since students will approach most of the problems differently, they must also state why they decided to approach the exercise as they did. Each grading period also has some type of student-centered project, which they are usually given several weeks to complete.

I also give in-class tests. Ninety percent of the test covers the material we have just finished studying, and 10 percent is review. There is usually a bonus problem involving multiple concepts. The problems require the students to show all their work for full credit. I start the year telling the students that the answer alone is only worth one or two points. Some of the problems require written answers or explanations. These tests are usually given in class, and some students require extra time.

Assessment Plan

My goal was to incorporate some other forms of assessment to judge how well my students were learning the material. My strategy was to use cooperative learning along with lectures. Beginning the second semester, along with cooperative learning, I planned to use observation and questioning, problem-based investigations, and performance-assessment tasks.

The reason I wanted to continue these strategies is that knowing the types of questions to ask strengthens the ability to evaluate students' thinking and reasoning. Posing questions that require the students to think about mathematics allows them the opportunity to discover and validate mathematical concepts, then to make connections within the mathematical curriculum and to other subjects (as well as to internalize their understanding). Problem-based investigations teach students to produce solutions to problems, not merely to recognize solutions. Since the take-home tests were multiple-exercise problems that required students to integrate new and previously learned concepts, I wanted to continue using this form of performance-based assessment.

The first day of the second semester, I formed the class into nine groups, seven with four members and two with three members. If this had been the first day of the school year, students would have exchanged phone numbers and addresses within each group and spent time becoming comfortable with each other. Since this was the second semester, the students were well acquainted, and we proceeded to discuss some of the different modes of assessment that would be used. We decided to work in groups every Tuesday and Thursday.

We discussed putting together portfolios, but somehow they never materialized. We then reviewed the process-based scoring schema we would use for the next grading period. The scoring system had three parts, each having three levels of achievement counting from one to four points. Therefore, students could receive up to twelve total points for a problem. The scoring system is as follows:

Understanding the problem
4 points — Complete understanding
2 or 3 points — Some difficulty
1 point — Poor understanding

Solution
4 points — Correct solution
2 or 3 points — Almost correct
1 point — Attempt

Explanation
4 points — Complete explanation
2 or 3 points — Incomplete explanation
1 point — Poor explanation

For the first few group sessions, I gave students two to three days' worth of definitions and some geometric concepts, and let them work the problems in their groups. I assigned higher-order problems that some students could not work by themselves; with the help of others in the group, they were successful. Groups were also used to review for tests. When someone was absent, the group provided him or her with what had been missed.

After their work on higher-order problems, I assigned a two-or three-concept problem for students to write up at home. If they had difficulty, they could use their notes, homework, or book, but they were on their honor not to discuss it between themselves. Their first take-home, write-up problem was one in which they had to establish that two triangles were similar and then use ratios to find an unknown length. These problems progressed in degree of difficulty. Two of the last problems assigned in the area and volume unit are given here.

1. The side of an equilateral triangle is s. A circle is inscribed in the triangle, and a square is inscribed in the circle. Find the area of the square.

2. A wooden form for a small dam is in the shape of a right prism whose base is an isosceles trapezoid as shown in the adjacent figure. AB is 3 feet, CD is 5 feet, h is 8 feet, and the dam is 44 feet long. The form has been filled with concrete to a depth of 2 feet. Find to the nearest cubic yard the additional number of cubic yards of concrete needed to fill the form.

Along with these problems, groups were also given a project to cut a color cartoon from the Sunday newspaper, construct a grid to cover the cartoon, then draw it five to twelve times the original size while preserving all similarity. The students also had to write about how they did their work, what problems they encountered, and what they did to overcome those technicalities.

I feel that had I started the students in groups from the beginning of the year, I would have had better reactions and results. It took me a long time to adjust to giving up control, except for guiding a group back on the path during those two days of the week. If I had more experience at group learning, I would also have exhibited a more positive attitude, which would have been reflected in my students. Most of these students started with negative feelings toward working in groups. With my inexperience as to what to expect or where to go, it was frustrating for both sides. However, the class and I became more adept at group work, and I feel it helped many individuals.

Some groups, of course, never learned how to work together. Instead, it was just four people sitting at the same table, all working individually and then checking their answers. Some groups learned to break certain problems into component parts and attack them separately, then bring the results together to solve the problem. In the discovery lessons on solids, certain groups split the work load, made their solids, and discovered the formulas for total surface area, lateral area, volume, and capacity before the groups working as individuals even finished their models. For the most part, students with lower grade averages did better working in groups, tended to learn concepts better, and improved their ability to write what they were doing. Students with higher averages tended to remain at the same level or decrease somewhat. Those students whose averages lowered a few points were quick to blame it on others in their group or on the group grade. However, everyone's individual grades were lower than any group grade.

After trying cooperative learning and overcoming my personal fears, I have found it to be an effective teaching strategy. First of all, all students must take an active role, both in doing the work (with everyone being responsible for their own part) and in judging each other's performance. Second, it allows the group to delve deeper into extensions that might seem impossible to some individuals. Third, it deemphasizes passive learning and teacher-dominated routine problem solving and encourages student participation in which reasoning and communicating are stressed.

Having students write out their work gives teachers another way to evaluate them. Students usually make calculations without explanations, and these often fail to reveal sufficiently the nature of their work and thinking. Writing out their work better conveys that thinking. Next year, I'm going to add portfolios to my assessment package so students will have a running record of their work and proof of their improvement. I am also going to expand these new strategies to my algebra classes.

Assessing Problem Solving in Fifth Grade
Carol Skaff
Stewart Elementary School

Huntsville, Texas, is situated on the far western edge of the great pine forest that reaches from the southern Atlantic coast to the Brazos River in east-central Texas. Huntsville's population numbers about thirty thousand, increasing significantly during the school year due to the twelve thousand students enrolled in Sam Houston State University (SHSU). This university is renowned for its teacher education and criminal justice departments. Within the community of Huntsville are located the central administrative offices of the Texas Department of Corrections (TDC). There are several major prisons of the TDC in and around Huntsville. Many children's parents are employed by TDC, SHSU, local businesses, the local logging industry, or ranches and farms.

Stewart Elementary is located in a residential area among towering east Texas pine trees. The population at Stewart Elementary includes 681 students and forty-three teachers. The student population comprises 65 percent white children, 19 percent Hispanic children, 15 percent African-American children, and 1 percent Asian children. Free or reduced-fee meal participants number 297, 43.6 percent of the total enrollment. Students are from predominantly low- to middle-income families. Our campus has an average of two transfers out of and two transfers into each classroom per year.

My fifth-grade classroom is made up of nineteen students: ten males and nine females. Fourteen of the students are white, three are African-American, and two are Hispanic. Three students consistently show high mathematical ability, twelve students show average ability, and four students show low computational ability. These same four students also scored at a nonmastery level on the mathematical portion of the 1991 Texas Assessment of Academic Skills Test. When assigning six-week math grades, I assess students on both ability and effort demonstrated in class. Due to ability-based grading, the four low-achieving students usually make a six-week grade of C or B-. This grade does not always reflect the low-achieving students' abilitities to reason mathematically.

The whole class, including the low-achieving students, enjoys mathematics and consistently puts forth its best effort. The class is motivated to solve mathematical problems, especially those requiring a process approach. Problem solving is the daily focus of math lessons in my classroom. Students begin class with a problem that emphasizes reasoning and higher-order thinking skills. As students begin their day, they prepare for class and immediately begin work on the problem of the day. Students are free to work cooperatively while solving that problem. Many students prefer to work independently; others gain confidence in knowing they may work with their group members.

After morning announcements and homeroom administrative chores, the whole class discusses the problem they have been working on that morning. I often call upon a student whom I have previously identified as having a unique or correct solution to the problem. This student then becomes the teacher and goes through the process that she or he used to come to the solution. This approach engages the whole class more than if I presented the answer. My role in the problem-of-the-day discussion is to help students learn to think about their own and others' thought processes. After the exercise has been discussed, I help the class understand the processes that led to the student's solution. The class's interest in solving mathematical problems has significantly increased as a result. Students feel successful when they achieve a correct or novel solution. They also begin to appreciate unique solutions to and unusual thinking about mathematical problems. The students look forward to the sharing step of the problem-solving process, and they feel a personal ownership of their math solutions.

After the problem of the day, I introduce and teach the daily lesson based upon the Huntsville Independent School District's fifth-grade math curriculum. After the lesson and guided practice, students work independently or cooperatively solving problems using the skills worked on for that day. Students who finish their work early are free to check their work. All work is due the following day at the beginning of math class.

On days when we do not have a formal lesson on new math skills, we often have an extended problem-solving activity. Students work collaboratively in pairs or in small groups of three to four to solve open-ended problems. As most groups finish their investigations, the whole class comes together to share and summarize findings and to finalize written responses to the problem-solving activity.

I assess children continuously during math instruction. Reteaching is done individually and immediately when learning problems are identified. Each student's work is monitored, reviewed, and scrutinized daily as it is turned in the next morning.

Cooperative groups are evaluated while they work together on open-ended math problems. The group is assessed on its collaborative skills and the quality of its verbal and written responses to a given activity. My students also keep a math portfolio into which they place self-selected problems of the day. This math portfolio is an ongoing visual representation of each student's growth in his or her problem-solving abilities.

Formal tests are infrequent, due to the organization and time restraints in my classroom. I feel that the intense exposure to daily problem solving and the quantity of math skills to be covered in the fifth grade leave little time for formal testing. Assessment does take place continuously during and at the end of learning units as outlined by my district's curriculum guide. I design my own instruments or modify those provided by my district in order to focus on students' growth in problem-solving and reasoning ability and proficiency in computation.

Tests in my room appear to be very much like a daily assignment.

The problem-solving tasks are like the problem of the day. Problem solving and computation are given about equal weight on a test. Cooperative group assessment activities are similar to the problems on which groups have worked on a daily basis. The test does not appear to be a unique or stressful experience for the students; it consists of much the same type of problem-solving situation and computation the students experience daily in class.

Alternative Assessment

When I began planning an alternative assessment program for my classroom, my goal was to use daily open-ended mathematical problems that would assist students to begin thinking about math in a new way. I hoped to use problems that would appeal to a broad cross section of students in the classroom. I felt that by using open-ended tasks, I would be able to engage high-achieving students, encourage average-ability math students to continue building their reasoning skills, and challenge low-achieving math students through these problems' nonthreatening nature and the cooperative atmosphere of the classroom. I stressed that answers were often less important than understanding the process by which they were developed. I emphasized mathematical process rather than products. I felt that students low in computational skills were able to show ability in mathematical problem solving. I wanted to remove the intimidation of computation and open up the problem-solving process so all students would have an opportunity to demonstrate an understanding of mathematical concepts.

The strategy of using the problem of the day and allowing students to verbalize their solutions to classmates created an open forum within the classroom where all students had an occasion to show their mathematical ability. I formally began using the problem of the day and cooperative math assessment activities after Christmas break. From January until May, I observed students' daily classroom work and monitored each student's math portfolio entries weekly. My goal was to be able to evaluate each student's growth in (1) mathematical problem solving using higher-order thinking skills and (2) ability to communicate effectively using mathematical terminology, both orally and in writing.

When designing the math assessment program, I intended to use a numerical grading system covering four criteria: original and creative thinking, pertinent strategies, solutions and extensions, and communication. I hoped to use a five-point rating scale to assess performance in each criterion, as follows:

5 — Strong ability in the criterion
4 — Commendable ability
3 — Average ability
2 — Below-average ability
1 — Little response within criterion

I planned to use the four criteria and the five-point rating scale as 50 percent of each student's total math grade.

When I began to implement this grading scale, the numbers seemed arbitrary and inappropriate to a student's performance and growth. Students had trouble adjusting to the new scale for grading work. Interpreting the scale to the students became laborious and confusing. Ultimately, I felt that the numerical grade would need to be adjusted to a percentage grade to be compatible with daily work grades. I dispensed with this form of scoring fairly quickly.

Each student's work from the problem of the day still went into a math portfolio. The portfolio allowed the student to track his or her individual growth and to claim ownership of that work. I relied upon cooperative group evaluation, individual open-ended testing instruments, and the individual math portfolios to make final assessments of students' growth in mathematical problem solving. As I modified my grading system to a conventional percentage-based measurement, students continued to produce outstanding and innovative solutions to problem solving and open-ended math activities. The class is still enthusiastic about solving the problem of the day. The students look forward to group problem-solving activities. The written responses to tasks continue to improve in organization and clarity. The class can verbalize and write the thinking processes that led to its solutions and extensions of problems.

I have seen tremendous growth in problem solving and in children's ability to communicate using effective mathematical terminology. A noteworthy difficulty in the problem-solving math class continues to be assigning a numerical grade to problem solving as a process rather than a product. I shall continue carefully to pace, monitor, and evaluate students' work in my problem-solving classroom. I will also investigate alternative methods of achieving a numerical assessment instrument that will allow me to translate holistically a student's math work based upon the creative thinking, use of problem-solving strategies, ability to achieve a correct solution and extend that solution into new areas of thought, and communication of thinking processes through skillful use of math terminology.

13

MODELS FOR HIGH SCHOOL

HIGH SCHOOL STUDENTS HAVE HAD MANY YEARS OF EXPERIENCE WITH THE traditional approaches to learning and doing mathematics, including how to be successful on tests. Many of these students have become comfortable with the learning sequence that in simplified form consists of "listen, practice, memorize, and recall for a test." They have been trained to include all of the steps in solving an equation and to show all (computational) work. Most students have not been required or requested to write or give verbal explanations of problem-solving processes. The idea of an assessment or grade based on anything except the correct answer is quite foreign.

For these reasons, making changes in something as critical as testing can be difficult in high school. Higher-ability students are often the most resistant to a change, since they have been successful under the traditional system. And as we saw earlier, if the assessment includes outcomes based on work in groups, there can be resentment that "lazy" or less able students will benefit unfairly.

It is essential in the high school grades to communicate early with the students about alternative assessment goals, involve them in planning, and implement new approaches gradually and on a trial basis before making permanent changes. The teachers in this project were persistent in helping their students realize the benefits of these new strategies. If one approach failed, they talked with colleagues, shared ideas, and tried another strategy. This pattern was especially important in encouraging high school students to write in journals about their solutions to math problems or the things they were learning. The examples in this chapter provide hints about what is possible to accomplish in alternative assessment at the high school level.

Assessment of Communication Skills in Algebra I
Dorothy Aiken
Moody High School

Moody High School is a small school in central Texas with about 170 students. Moody is a rural community, and many students are bused in from surrounding areas. Approximately 10 percent of the students are African-American, and 17 percent are Hispanic. Many of my students are of a lower socioeconomic status. This community has not traditionally valued education, although this situation may be changing. Sports and agricultural activities receive a lot of attention from the students and are supported actively by the community. For many, education does not seem to be so important as athletic endeavors.

The group participating in this project was a first-year algebra class composed of thirteen girls in the eighth through eleventh grades. One girl transferred from out of state just last week. Four of the girls are Hispanic; the rest are white. One ninth-grade student is married and has a baby. Several of the girls have poor attendance records. One student, who transferred to Moody in November, has profound hearing loss in both ears. The migrant teacher is working to locate money for hearing aids for her. The girls are active in sports, cheerleading, and agriculture.

The girls have varying abilities in math. One of the eighth graders and two of the ninth graders do very well; others have average or lower abilities, and the girl with the hearing loss does very poorly. We do not have a record of how long she has had the loss; however, since she has a speech problem, I suspect that she may have had it from an early age. The girls interact well together, and it is a very pleasant class. They enjoy helping each other. Like any normal teenagers, they would rather socialize than work on algebra.

I have no opportunity to use team teaching. I teach the majority of the math classes at the high school, including algebra I, algebra II, informal geometry, trigonometry, and precalculus. No other teacher teaches these subjects. There are three teachers who teach geometry and prealgebra part-time. I see them very little and miss being able to collaborate on ideas.

My teaching includes lecture, questions and answers, and group work. The students work on homework together and use peer tutoring. The students have assignments almost daily. They have weekly quizzes and chapter tests. These are used for assigning grades, and they supply information for reteaching. The students also write journal entries, which provide insight into their problems and strengths.

Assessment Plan

My goal was to increase the ability of the students to communicate their ideas and thinking processes and to enable them to clarify their thinking by verbalizing orally and in writing. It was my hope that this approach would increase their success in mathematics. To implement this plan, the students wrote frequent journal entries, which they kept in their algebra notebooks. Early in the year, I gave them a list of topics to be addressed for a general journal entry. These included

- What was today's lesson about?
- What did you like about the assignment?
- What are some of your questions about the lesson?
- How did your methods for solving the problems differ from those of your classmates?
- What was the hardest part of this lesson?

The students were directed to write their journals in complete sentences with complete thoughts. Sometimes, the students were asked to explain how to solve a specific problem. After much frustration with the product I received, I directed them to write a letter to a friend. These were the guidelines:

> A friend asked for your help in solving problem _____ . You didn't have time then to help. Later, you wrote a letter to explain the problem. Make this an informal letter that explains the process completely. If another teacher took this letter from you, she should have no trouble understanding exactly what you are talking about.

On two occasions, the students wrote personal biographies. The first was written on the first day of class. The second was composed toward the end of the first semester and included students' math backgrounds, their likes and dislikes, their hobbies, and their long-term goals educationally, vocationally, and avocationally.

The students would occasionally assess each other's writing. During the second semester, I conducted personal interviews. Also about this time, I began keeping a record of positive behaviors I observed. Later, I included a writing assessment on each test.

The journal entries generally improved over time. Some students still had to be reminded to write complete sentences with complete thoughts and to introduce the topic they were discussing. In explaining a specific problem, the letter-writing approach has improved the outcome tremendously. Some students will write a very friendly, chatty letter, and the writing is almost always done with more clarity than when they are just asked to write an explanation of how to solve the problem. In assessing the writing of others, they gained a better understanding of how to make their writing express their ideas to others.

I enjoyed the personal interviews with the students, but I did not have any great revelations. Because Moody is such a small school and this is such a small, informal class in which the students feel free to talk, I was not surprised at any of the information I received.

In an attempt to evaluate cooperative work on solving problems, I developed a checklist of behaviors to observe. The chart for positive behaviors included each student's name and a column for

- Working cooperatively
- Being supportive of others
- Volunteering during class discussions
- Demonstrating leadership
- Extending or connecting learning

The chart seemed like a good idea in the beginning, but because this class interacts so well, I would have needed to spend all my time keeping the chart in order to be accurate. I considered omitting some of the behaviors they exhibited consistently, but these exclusions would have altered the intentions of keeping the record. If only those behaviors that dealt directly with the math assignment were included, the records would have been weighted heavily in favor of those students who did well on any standard measurement; I might have been just creating another opportunity for some of the slower students to do less well. In the end, the students received a cumulative grade for journals and for positive behavior, encouraging them to continue to work together; however, I had to limit the time I kept the record. I do think the chart might be very useful for a class that does not interact well naturally.

Written work on tests did not prove very successful. Few students wrote very good responses. I think I need to start with the writing much earlier in the year, and I need to gain more experience in composing appropriate questions.

Initially, the students rejected the idea of writing journals. The general response was, "This is algebra. Why do we have to write?" They gradually accepted the journal without complaint, and they became much better at communicating their ideas. Some liked to write their journals on the computer; others preferred to write them in longhand. Some resisted writing their personal biographies, but I found them very interesting and felt that I understood the girls better as persons, not just as algebra students. They generally told me more about themselves in writing than they did in interviews; however, I think the interviews conveyed to them that they could talk to me on a personal level.

I believe that I have become more aware of the processes that students go through in solving problems. I realize that arriving at a correct answer is not the only measure of their abilities. In the past, I have given partial credit for work with incorrect answers, but now I have a method of giving credit for other abilities that are needed in the real world. I will try to continue to find ways to assess mathematical abilities and thinking.

I believe that working to improve communication skills in mathematics is a worthwhile goal and that this year's efforts have been somewhat successful. Unfortunately, these methods have not dramatically improved my students' abilities in math. Those who already did well in math were better able to communicate their thinking; those who struggled with math also had trouble with the specific writing assignments — but they improved. I will continue to use writing and oral communication in my classes and feel confident that these will be helpful to me and my students. I will try to extend the efforts further.

I would recommend that teachers who want to implement some of these methods introduce them gradually. It is difficult to make numerous changes all at once. I hope that next year I will have the experience to make communication a more effective tool in my classroom.

Assessment of Problem Solving in Algebra I
Dorothy Albrecht
La Grange High School

La Grange is the county seat of Fayette County. It is a small, friendly town with a population of just under four thousand. Until a few years ago, most of the students in the school system had roots in Fayette County. With the construction of the Fayette Power Project and a mini–oil boom, however, the population has changed considerably. More and more of the students are relative newcomers to the area.

Many of the younger students are bused from the rural area surrounding La Grange, whereas a large population of the high school commutes by either private automobile or bus. The high school generally has an enrollment of approximately five hundred. Seventy-seven percent of these students are white (many of German or Czech heritage). Hispanics and African-Americans each make up approximately 11 percent of our student body.

The class that has been the target for this course is algebra I, which now has twenty-three students. Of these, one is a junior, four are sophomores, and the other eighteen are freshmen. All of the upper classmen are boys; ten of the students are girls. One of the students is in our gifted and talented program. The class has one African-American and two Hispanic students. Three of the students are members of our newly organized math club, and most of the freshmen are in some extracurricular activity, mostly athletics or band. The majority of the students would like to do as little as possible and still receive credit for the course. A few have high expectations and go the extra mile.

Except on major test days, class is usually begun with a warm-up exercise. This might be a problem similar to the previous assignment, an introduction to the day's lesson, a review of a statewide assessment test objective, something on spatial relations or logical reasoning, or a nonroutine problem. Five percent of the six-week grade is based on the students' attempts at these problems. Answers are not the basis for grading; student involvement is the determining factor. A variety of teaching strategies are used: lecture, demonstration, question and answer, group activity, cooperative learning, peer tutoring, board work, and some computer work.

Assignments are made frequently. Some are individual and some are group activities; most are short-term assignments due the following day. These are used in several ways. Sometimes, I collect them, check them myself, and assign a grade. Other times, the students check them themselves, marking their errors. The assignments are then collected, and a completion or effort grade is given. On occasions, the student is requested to mark those problems that he or she feels most comfortable with. These problems are then graded in detail, and the remainder are treated as completion problems.

I ask students to keep a notebook of daily assignments and class notes. The notes might be copies of examples given to demonstrate a conceptual definition, rules, or the student's observations. They may take many forms. The thing I am looking for is whether or not the student has something to help her or him solve problems. Tests are used to evaluate the students' knowledge and my teaching. The results of these are often the determining factor for warm-up assignments as well as reteaching topics.

Assessment Plan

A combination of reasons has caused me to choose problem solving as the area in which to use innovative teaching and assessment. While we all know that word problems are not the best examples of problem solving, they do pose difficulties, both real and imaginary. Many of my students will not even attempt to solve the word-problem portion of a test or quiz. However, with national and state standards mandating (as well as the real world insisting) that our students be problem solvers, this seems to be the place I am most needed in helping my students.

For some time, I have used the traditional five-step method of solving these problems: read the problem carefully and decide what is given and what is asked, define the variables and write an equation, solve the equation, check for reasonableness, and write a conclusion. Even when students used tables, diagrams, guessing and checking, or working backwards, I still expected to see the steps just outlined.

My plan now is to be much more flexible in what I will accept as problem solving as well as to include many more opportunities for using problem solving in my classroom. Many of my warm-up exercises are spatial or what are considered nonroutine problems. These may be solved in small groups or individually using any means available to the students. Assessment on these exercises is based solely upon their attempted solution. No one is denied credit for not getting the correct solution. The idea is to tempt students to try problem solving.

As my algebra I course progressed, I included more and more word problems in daily exercises, quizzes, and tests. These problems were not all of one type (for example, all mixture problems, all rate problems, all digit or coin problems) but were varied; many were real-life situations in which students might find themselves. The students could not simply ignore these problems because their grade would be substantially jeopardized.

This was not an attempt to cause failure but to ensure that the problems were not overlooked. Since this was an algebra class, the instructions were, solve in any manner you choose, showing your work in a manner that can be followed by me or a fellow student; write an equation to represent this problem; conclude with a statement of your solution and why you believe it to be the solution. To assess this work, I used a rating system similar to the six-level scale from *Assessment Alternatives in Mathematics* (Stenmark, 1989). I changed the scale from the original six points to a twelve-point maximum in order to give a greater range between the best and poorest papers.

Demonstrated Competence
12 points — Exemplary response
10 points — Competent response

Satisfactory Response
8 points — Minor flaws but satisfactory
6 points — Serious flaws but nearly satisfactory

Inadequate Response
4 points — Begins but fails to complete problem
2 points — Unable to begin effectively
0 points — No attempt

To introduce problem-solving strategies and the scoring system, I adapted word problems so that students would focus on the data and the question being asked, rather than jumping into trying to find an answer. For example, I provided the equation for a problem and asked the students to solve it. I then asked them to use the equation to fill in the missing information. Finally, they gave the solution to the problem.

> 1. Curtis has _____ more quarters in his collection than Sharon has in hers. Together, they have _____ quarters. How many quarters does Sharon have?
> *Equation:* $q + q + 50 = 190$

This approach helped the students see the connection between the information given in the problem and in the equation. The scoring rubric allowed me to give credit for the work they were able to do successfully.

A second approach was to provide the information in a word problem but leave out the question. The students were asked to write at least two questions that could be answered using this information. Here is an example.

> 2. It is 200 miles from Houston to San Antonio. About halfway between the two cities is Schulenburg. Mary usually drives her small foreign car the speed limit on the interstate. Susan drives her Le Baron convertible faster than Mary by about 5 miles per hour.

Especially when they are working in groups, I do not hear nearly so many complaints as before about word problems. More of them on quizzes and tests are being attempted now. But still, students are reluctant to write conclusions to these problems. In their minds, they have the answer. What more can I, the teacher, want?

As a result of this project, I am even more conscious of the need for problem-solving skills and put more emphasis on the variety of methods that may be used in problem solving. Also, it is not important that all students solve a problem in the same way. What matters is that the student understands what he or she is doing and whether the conclusion reached is a justifiable one. Students should be made aware of my expectations as well as those of the real world. More emphasis should be placed on problem-solving situations rather than solving an equation or simplifying a mathematical expression. An early attempt should be made to help students overcome their objections to word problems. They need to see the relevance of this skill in their everyday lives. Teachers should not skimp on using these problems because they are harder or take more time to evaluate.

It is my hope that these approaches will help make my students better, as well as more willing, problem solvers. I will continually remind them of the need for looking carefully at the information in a problem and to find the connection between the information and the question asked. I hope they will learn to recognize when necessary data are missing, as well as when more information is given than is needed.

Assessing Student-Formulated Problems in Algebra I
Olivia Allen
Langham Creek High School

Langham Creek High School is a suburban high school located in the northwest part of Houston, Texas. It is one of four high schools in the school district, with an enrollment of approximately 2,300 students. The student body is becoming more culturally diverse. During the current school year, 65 percent of the students are white, 14 percent are Hispanic, 9 percent are African-American, 9 percent are Asian, and the remainder are of various other backgrounds. The number of students who qualify for a free or reduced-price lunch is steadily increasing. This number is more than 12 percent of the current enrollment.

The group I used for alternative assessment was an algebra I class. Eighteen students were white, seven students were Hispanic, and five students were African-American, with an equal number of male and female students. The class is the only algebra I L class that I teach. The L is a label used by the school district to denote those students who were below level in their eighth-grade math class or who were enrolled in a prealgebra class the year before.

Classroom organization is very important to me, and one might say that

I am very structured. Students are arranged in a specific seating arrangement; each student is paired with someone else. I rotate the seating arrangement on a biweekly basis, so that partners change. I have been fortunate to have an equal number of males and females in this class, so I always pair each student with someone of the opposite sex. The students like the pairing and appreciate the fact that I rotate them regularly. This system has given them the opportunity to work with many different individuals with varying abilities.

The class period is divided into several segments. I begin with problems written on the overhead projector. I demonstrate different means of working these after giving students an appropriate amount of time to solve them. If there are questions about homework, I will answer them. Again, I vary my method of checking homework. I may have students write certain problems on the board, grade the homework in class, or just ask them to hand it in for me to grade. I then teach the new lesson, working through several example problems, and allow students to work problems prior to giving them the assignment. Because students will rarely do homework outside of the classroom, most assignments are due before the end of the period. Some of these students have jobs after school or responsibilities at home and do no homework. Students usually work on their assignments with their partners. These students need a lot of motivation, so it is important to vary the instruction. Games are used for reviews, and access to the computer lab has become most exciting for these students.

The six teachers on the algebra I L team meet on a weekly basis to plan lessons for the ensuing week. We decide which sections of each chapter will be covered, as well as which problems are to be worked. A test is developed by the group and given on the same day in all classes. Tests are given every one to two weeks. Within every six-week marking period, usually four to five tests count as 67 percent of the grade. Most tests consist of problems comparable to the ones in the textbook. Partial credit is often given on these tests. The team decides the amount and criteria for partial credit, as all teachers must grade by the same standard. At the end of the six weeks is a comprehensive exam. Multiple-choice tests are most often written for this purpose. The rest of the grade is determined by quizzes and homework. Each teacher may choose the manner in which to determine this last third of the students' grade.

Assessment Plan

Students rarely have the opportunity to make up their own problems in mathematics. I feel that if the students understand the concepts that have been taught, they should be able to write a problem of their own. This is my goal of alternative assessment. Its purpose is to determine whether students can merely reproduce problems exactly like those worked in class or whether they can transfer the knowledge and write a unique problem based upon the material learned.

Given that the students had worked in pairs since almost the beginning of the school year, I had them make up a problem for their partners and then solve their own problem on a separate sheet of paper. When both finished, they handed them in. I used process-based scoring to assess how each problem was written, the solution given by the creator of the problem, and the solution given by the partner. The process-based scoring system was as follows:

Understanding the Concept
4 points—Complete understanding
2 points—Some understanding
1 point—Poor understanding

Solution of the Problem
4 points—All correct
2 points—Partially correct
1 point—Attempted to solve

Creativity of the Problem
4 points—Completely different from text
2 points—Somewhat different from text
1 point—Comparable to types in text

Solution of Partner's Problem
4 points—Completely correct
2 points—Partially correct
1 point—Attempted to solve

This process was done on a weekly basis beginning with the second semester and was incorporated as a daily grade. Since I usually take between fifteen and twenty homework and quiz marks per six weeks to be used for one-third of the grade, the process-based scoring was not a highly significant part of their grade. However, the students were very excited when we began the alternative assessment. I usually did this at the end of the period. When I first started, the students would nearly always write a problem comparable to the ones used in class that day. Also, although they understood the process of what I expected of them, quite a few of them did not write instructions. In these cases, students asked their partners what was expected of them. As an example, a problem was written as $3x^2 + 13x - 10 = 0$. The student could merely want his partner to list the coefficient to be used in the quadratic formula or the partner could want the problem solved by using that formula.

When we covered the unit on graphing equations of lines, the problems that some of the students wrote were impossible to solve, even though I had made graph paper available to those who chose to write a problem requiring its use. The problems written had y-intercepts that far exceeded the graph paper. The section on solving systems of equations also produced some disastrous results when the students were asked to solve by graphing. The problems in the text always had points of intersection that had integer values. I had stated to the students that graphing was only effective if there was a point of intersection that was an integer. However, when some wrote their problems, they did not take this fact into consideration; in those cases, even the students who had written the problems were unable to solve them. If the student was expected to solve a system of equations by substitution, most (both the person who wrote the problem as well as the partner) also had difficulty if there were fractional answers. In some cases, the partner merely stated that the problem could not be solved.

The resulting grades were not good. More than half the students received a failing grade, which consisted of the average of those grades taken for the process-based scoring. At this point, I wondered whether I had graded too harshly. The next time I used the alternative assessment, I explained in detail what parts were important in the process. Since we were studying exponents, I hoped the results would be better since the students seemed to be having an easier time with this unit. The results were avarage, but the same problems existed as before—that is, the students did not write instructions; some tried to make problems too difficult and could not solve their own problems; or the problems just did not make any sense.

The grades at the end of the next six-week grading period produced similar results. It was at this time that students began to complain about writing their own problems. It was becoming increasingly evident that those students who performed the worst on the "regular" tests were the same ones to score the least number of points on the process-based scoring system. The most obvious concern of most students was that their partners would write a problem that was too difficult to be solved. If this was the case, the person who wrote the problem usually had difficulty solving the problem as well.

This system of scoring should prove to be effective if students are given more time to become accustomed to it. This would probably alleviate the complaints because the students saw the process-based scoring as being something different. If used on a regular basis and for a longer period, the students would think of it not as being something different but rather as part of the process of how they were graded.

Assessment of Discovery Learning in Informal Geometry
Beth Douglass
Langham Creek High School

Langham Creek High School is part of the Cypress-Fairbanks Independent School District and is located in northwest Houston, home to a diverse population. To the southeast of the school, there are many rental homes and apartments that are occupied for short periods of time. To the southwest of the school, the community is middle to upper class. Langham Creek High School is seven years old. The student population has grown rapidly over the last few years. We have just about reached capacity with about 2,195 students.

The ethnicity of the school is about 65 percent whites, 14 percent Hispanics, 9 percent African-Americans, and 12 percent Asians and other minorities.

My alternative assessment project was conducted in an informal geometry class consisting of twenty students, eight males and twelve females. The ethnic makeup of the class was twelve whites, four African-Americans, three Hispanics, and one Asian. Informal geometry is considered a sophomore-level course; out of the twenty students, sixteen were in the tenth grade, and the rest were in the eleventh grade. These students were previously unsuccessful in mathematics. The majority of the students did not enjoy mathematics and were not easily motivated. Moreover, 70 percent of the students held afterschool jobs and therefore were often tired during first period. On tests, they performed best when only one or two topics had been covered. The retention of mathematics for these students was poor, and if asked to use previous knowledge, they tended to run into difficulty. The students enjoyed playing games and working in groups. When they were in charge of their own learning or when the lesson related to everyday life, they seemed to get excited about mathematics. The students generally tried hard during class though they rarely returned complete homework assignments. As long as there was someone to push them to do the work, however, they would get the work done.

Cypress-Fairbanks school district encourages the use of team planning. At the high school level, if there are ten or more sections of a subject, a team leader is designated to act as a facilitator. The team works together to plan lessons and write tests. As a team, we are required to teach the same topics on the same day. We are also required to give the same test to all informal geometry students. We usually cover one topic per day, but we have the option to teach more or less material in a given period of time. I have concentrated on using manipulatives on a regular basis in my classroom. The students also seem to enjoy the lessons when hands-on materials are incorporated.

The students in the informal geometry class were given a wide array of assignments: worksheets, quizzes, group work, projects, puzzles, and tests. Since the informal geometry textbook is simply a geometry textbook without proofs, I relied on supplementary materials. The students did not use their textbooks because most of the problems would have had to be modified. The supplemental material included worksheets, puzzles, and quizzes. The school encouraged us to give multiple-choice exams so that the students could have practice taking this particular type of test. Every six weeks, the students were required to complete a project outside of class, which counted as a test grade.

Assessment Plan

The knowledge assessed in the classroom was inductive reasoning, using an informal guided-discovery approach and process-based scoring. The students worked with the tools of geometry to discover geometric properties by experimentation and observation. In the process, the students were encouraged to take responsibility for their own learning and to participate. Using inductive reasoning, the students were required to write their own definitions, discover relationships, and solve both standard and nonstandard problems. This approach also placed emphasis on the process of problem solving, not simply on the solutions to an exercise.

The students were evaluated in two different ways. The first was for their work in groups. The students were given a particular role and had to carry out the responsibilities of that job. The roles were facilitator, thinker, supporter, and questioner. Each person could receive up to twenty points every time he or she worked in groups. Five of these scores would contribute to one grade worth one hundred points. The students were also assessed using process-based scoring. The students were given a grade for working one of two problems every week that they had not previously seen. A scoring sheet was used to give the student a grade based upon three factors:

Understanding the Problem
4 points — Complete understanding
2 points — Some difficulty
1 point — Poor understanding

Solution
4 points — Correct solution
2 points — Almost correct
1 point — Attempt

Explanation
4 points — Complete explanation
3 points — Incomplete explanation
1 point — Poor explanation

Students who understood the problem and could explain how they arrived at the solution could still score high without arriving at the correct answer. They were thereby encouraged to think about the process instead of just focusing on the correct answer.

My goal for alternative assessment was to allow the students to learn by doing. With the use of manipulative materials, this objective can be accomplished. Determining a way to assess the students also led me to cooperative learning. The ability to make conjectures in geometry requires high-level thinking skills and can produce anxiety when a student works alone. Working with other students reduces this stress. Cooperative learning allows the students to become more active and involved in the learning process. It also focuses on the process instead of strictly on the result. Thus, this technique was used when assessing students on their knowledge of geometric concepts. Process-based scoring gave them the opportunity to explain how they arrived at their conclusions, instead of evaluating their knowledge solely on the answer.

I originally planned to grade the students on their ability to arrive at the desired geometric definition without any help from me. The students would brainstorm with their groups to arrive at the definition. I soon discovered that these students often needed help or hints to lead them in the right direction. So I changed my method and allowed each group to ask me two questions when we were doing discovery lessons in groups. The students made sure they could not go any further without my help before they used a question "coupon."

The students were apprehensive about my assessment plan. They were most comfortable and secure with a routine. Even when I rearranged the desks in my room, it upset their routine. The students did not want to try anything new at the beginning of my assessment period and often asked me, "Why are we doing this?" After approximately three weeks of the cooperative learning, their attitudes seemed to change. They were excited about working in groups and especially excited about using manipulatives. Unfortunately, their attitudes toward the process-based scoring never changed. They thought that showing their process was unnecessary extra work. The students who did not show their work on their tests or on their homework assignments did not do well on this assessment. The students complained about the process-based scoring until the end.

My attitude toward the alternative assessment project is positive. The students seemed to be interested in mathematics and enjoyed the learning process. I have concluded that it was the teaching method that produced this enthusiasm. The students liked working with their hands and could accomplish tasks they would not have been able to do with paper and pencil. The alternative assessment allowed me to give a grade for using the manipulatives that otherwise I would not have awarded. Previously, I only gave grades for worksheets or homework that showed they could apply what they learned in class. The students were not threatened by the use of manipulatives or cooperative learning. They knew what their roles were and how I was grading them.

I will continue to use manipulatives and discovery learning in my mathematics classroom. Using a method to gauge the learning process encourages everyone to participate. It also enables the students to have daily grades other than strictly quizzes and homework and helps those who normally do not complete homework assignments. They have other grades to balance out their average.

I would like to continue using process-based scoring in my mathematics classroom although it was not very successful with this particular group of students. I feel that it would be more effective if I introduced it at the beginning of the school year. A routine would be established, and the students would have a better attitude toward the process. I liked using process-based scoring because I could see on paper exactly what the students were thinking. It allowed me to determine the method the students used to solve the problem. It also permitted me to see what each student did and did not understand. But, as previously mentioned, the students who did not do well on their homework and quizzes unfortunately did not do well on the process-based scoring. They refused to show their work and preferred to get a low score. Since these students were not easily motivated, they did not do well with paper-and-pencil assignments.

Overall, I feel that the alternative assessment project was a success with my students. Their attitudes toward mathematics became more positive than at the beginning of the school year. The students learned that there is more to mathematics than pencil and paper and enjoyed this learning process. It is a joy for a teacher to hear a student say, "Math is fun."

Writing Assessment Strategies in Algebra II
Fran Herron
Langham Creek High School

Langham Creek High School is located in a suburb of Houston. The population comes from two categories. Probably half of the students come from middle- to upper-middle-class families living in two subdivisions; most of the parents have white-collar jobs. The other half comes from areas with many apartment complexes and rental homes. From this area come more blue-collar workers, many with a high mobility rate. It is not unusual for our students to leave at some time during the year and sometimes return later. There are about 2,300 students in the school. Sixty-five percent are white, 14 percent Hispanic, 9 percent African-American, 9 percent Asian, and 3 percent other.

The alternative assessment I have chosen has been implemented with an algebra II class that has fluctuated between twenty and twenty-five students all year. Of the twenty-four enrolled now, sixteen are white, one is African-American, two are Indian, and five are Hispanic. This class is below level, and most students have very weak mathematical skills. One of the biggest obstacles to overcome with this class has been very low motivation and extreme lack of self-confidence. The students work for tangible rewards like candy and homework passes. Grades alone are not good motivators for these students.

In this class, I have received little parental support. The absentee rate is a big problem. Often, the absences are due to the students being on in-school suspension. For example, during the fifth six-week period, 28 percent of the students were absent an average of 31 percent of the time. Another 24 percent were absent 13 percent of the time. During the course of the year, I have had five students move in and seven withdraw. These numbers do not include several students who moved in and out simply because of schedule changes.

The organization of my classroom is rather structured. A typical day begins with a warm-up problem. Then we check homework and answer questions. I present new material with guided practice throughout, and then it is time to begin independent practice. On the average, I try to do group work two to three times per week, discovery work one time per week, computer lab practice one to two times per six weeks, and some sort of fun activity like a game or challenging problem two times per week. I use questioning constantly in my room. "I don't know" is not an acceptable answer to any question. I am constantly asking "why?" after students' responses to try and get them to think more. Our school operates under team planning so that we all follow the same schedule and give the same tests. This system is very helpful for sharing ideas but does not always allow for much flexibility.

An average assignment consists of fifteen to twenty minutes of practice four times per week. It is used to monitor progress and reinforce concepts. Tests are given every week or week and a half. The tests are very objective, and partial credit is often given. I have, of course, looked at some other methods throughout the year. The tests cover the basic "need to know" material. Though "nice to know" things are taught, they are not frequently tested. The tests are used to measure learning.

Assessment Plan

The students in this class as a whole are not concerned with the why or how of what they are doing but focus more on attaining the correct answer. The purpose of the assessment plan was thus to take the focus off the answer and to concentrate more on the importance of the process and on their understanding of the algebraic concept. The primary method of evaluating students' understanding of the mathematical processes was through writing. These writing assignments were to have three purposes, the first being diagnostic. By having students write down their prior knowledge, the pace of the class could be planned according to the needs of the students. The second and most important purpose of the assessment was to emphasize the algebraic processes. By writing, I hoped that they would have a new window through which to look at the processes they were learning; they could focus on how to get to the answer and why the process worked rather than concentrating on the end result. The third purpose of the plan was to create an overall evaluation of what the students had learned in order to readjust teaching techniques and pacing. This plan was to be implemented over the course of one semester.

Several types of assessment items were to be used in the plan. One was a daily journal. A list of concepts was to be given at the beginning of each day, and the students were to write what they knew about the concepts. At the end of the lesson, the students were to again write in their journals to record any knowledge gained that would help them understand the concepts. They were then to summarize either a process emphasized that day or one associated with a previously mastered concept.

Another assessment approach was to have the students write how the use of manipulatives compared or related to the algebraic concept being taught or reinforced. The students also had items on their tests focused on the processes learned. These items were of two types. One was specific algebra concepts learned in the unit being tested. The other included open-ended questions geared to the solution process.

The journals were to be graded once a week, with students graded on different days; the writing was to be a required ongoing process, not a last-minute effort. In addition to the journal entries, the manipulative comparisons were to be graded either on an individual basis or as a group effort, depending on the nature of the activity (as manipulatives are often used in a cooperative learning setting). The final assessment of an algebraic concept was to be made by standard tests with process-based scoring items.

To begin implementing the plan, I had students keep a journal. I started with simple warm-up problems on which they could be successful. The following is an example:

a. Solve $2x + 3 = 4$; then explain the process in writing.
b. $2(3 - 6*5)$ What is the first step in evaluating this expression?
c. How would you solve any two-step equation?
d. Explain how to graph a point.

Students were fairly successful and open to the idea. Some had to be prompted, especially when the questions became more generalized. It was hard to monitor all students. Those who were stuck without the opportunity to get help simply did not complete the assignment. I revised the generalized questioning so that students could work with a partner to answer the questions. This approach worked much better because students were able to ask and support each other.

My first approach—to assess preknowledge and postknowledge writing—did not work very well. Students could tell me orally what they knew about a concept but had a hard time putting it in writing. The greatest difficulty was in distinguishing which new concepts they had learned during the lesson. Some simply rewrote their notes. Their frustration level became so high that I abandoned the idea.

Writing was a good assessment for discovery learning, which once again worked best in groups. One example of its use was with graphing lines. Students had to draw a conclusion on how to tell where a line crossed the y-axis without graphing it. I learned that it was extremely important to be tolerant of "incorrect" terminology. I had to be very careful to grade the correct connection instead of incorrect terminology. However, I realized from this assessment that I needed to use the correct algebra term and the terms they understood interchangeably much more frequently; for example, they needed to switch to "constant" from "back number," and to "coefficient" from "number with x." This practice has produced a big improvement in vocabulary throughout the year. This type of assessment also helped me in later assignments to see that vocabulary needed to be emphasized in the algebra processes.

On the first major test, students were able to choose one of three problems on process writing that they had previously seen. Students who normally scored high on tests did well on the writing section; students who normally scored poorly on tests did not have a high success rate. I felt that the writing we had done may have helped them learn the material better, but they did not benefit from it on the test. Some left the problems blank.

My second approach was to use the assessment on homework. Students were instructed never to leave a problem blank. If they could not arrive at what seemed to be a "correct" answer, they were to write down everything they knew about the problem or concept for some partial credit. This system worked best for problems with more than one step. For example, simplifying exponent problems did not work very well since most solutions included only one step. Factoring and solving equations were more appropriate, as several steps applied to these problems.

I tried the same approach with my algebra II class, an on-level and more motivated group of students. They really liked it. I'm not sure if it was easier for them because writing made it more possible to identify familiar characteristics of difficult problems or if it was effective because they were more concerned with their grades. I think it was some of both. I have continued using this with my algebra II students and will continue in the future. In algebra I, I will work on some modifications. I did note that the algebra I students' attitudes toward this type of writing were much better than those in algebra II; the first group seemed to view it as being more beneficial.

My third and probably most helpful approach was to have students write or formulate their own algorithm for solving a type of problem or to create their own set of rules for a specific type of problem. Students seemed to understand the material better if they paired with someone to write the processes or rules in their own terms. One of the most effective was the exponents unit. I gave the students five sets of problems, each focusing on a specific concept. The students wrote their own rules for each set. I graded them to make sure the rules were correct and then returned them for the students to use as study guides or guidelines. This system also worked well for writing a set of rules for simplifying radicals (addition, subtraction, multiplication, division, and rationalizing the denominator).

One success I had was with my ESL (English-as-a-second-language) students. I had to be very understanding with the language barrier and very lenient in grading. However, I think this group really benefited from the writing. The students grew to understand the concepts better because they were forced to write their ideas down, an activity that required much more thought than simply working the problems. They seemed to have a positive outlook about this also.

Throughout the plan, I thus had several successes and several failures. My first goal was to evaluate students through their writings, but this diagnostic approach was not very successful since the students did not give me an accurate picture of what they knew. Not only was the assessment inaccurate, but the students' attitudes toward writing became negative because they did not see any personal advantages from it. As previously stated, this approach might work if it was started at the beginning of the year and if students helped to teach each other more.

The second goal of the plan was to have students focus on the algebraic processes they were learning. This was the area where I experimented most and that was the most successful. Three things resulted from the assessment. First, students' mathematical vocabulary improved, and I realized the importance of mixing my terms with ones they understood. Students' attitudes toward this type of assessment were much better because they saw it as more beneficial. Second, they were able to help each other in increasing their understanding of concepts. The third advantage was to give those students who needed, or those who would use it, their own personalized study guide in words that they would comprehend. I would definitely recommend having students write down their own sets of rules or their own algorithms.

Something I added to the plan during the course of its implementation was writing on homework assignments. This was very effective, and I recommend it for all levels. In general, I think the plan was an overall success, not necessarily as an assessment but as a teaching tool. I also think the plan would have worked better with a more motivated group of students and a more stable class with fewer absences and less mobility.

Assessment of Communication Ability in Honors Geometry
Mary Newberg
Montgomery High School

The community in which this school is located is seventy miles from downtown Houston and immediately adjacent to the suburban Houston community. The school district is a geographically large one, covering approximately 251 square miles. The area that feeds the school is composed of many diverse communities. The school district has grown from a small rural community school in which the ethnic makeup was evenly divided between white and African-American students to a large suburban one in which the minority population, mainly African-American, composes about 17 percent of the whole. There is a great diversity of socioeconomic status and life-style. Some students live on farms or in the country, and many parents are involved in agricultural occupations. The high school currently has 650 students enrolled. About 16 percent are considered of low socioeconomic status. Eighteen percent of all students are identified as gifted and talented. The size of the school and its diversity are positive influences; everyone knows and is known by everyone else.

The class that I chose as the pilot class for the assessment project is an honors geometry class. The class consists of twenty-four students, thirteen females and eleven males. Some are high achievers; all have considerable ability. Parental expectations and pressure are high. This class was chosen because it was my opinion that younger students would adapt more easily than older students to innovative and new ideas. Also, the ninth and tenth graders are not as driven by class ranking and grade points as are eleventh and twelfth graders. In addition, geometry seemed to be an ideal course to begin alternative assessment techniques because it readily lends itself to models, projects, diagrams, and manipulatives. Feedback from students about concepts traditionally taught in geometry indicated a belief that geometry was memorizing theorems, proofs, and postulates but had no relation to the real world of work. I determined that this geometry class would be different.

My teaching style is student-centered. Whenever possible, I allow students to work in cooperative groups in order to discover a principle, theorem, or postulate. The groups are chosen at random, and every student has a job to do. I keep lecturing to a minimum and use student examples for modeling. Students are assigned outside research projects, as individuals and in groups, so they can make connections to geometry in real life. All assignments are made at the beginning of each six-week grading period, and tests are given either weekly or every two weeks. The types of assignments include cooperative group work, manipulative exercises, extended problem solving, review sheets, and review of already-covered concepts and of algebra concepts. Homework and manipulative or group work are not graded except for completion. One or two objectives are tested weekly with corrections or extensions as needed. The student then has an opportunity to be tested again on any objective not mastered.

Assessment Plan

The initial plan for implementation of alternative strategies called for assessment of two elements of learning according to the NCTM *Standards:* communication and problem solving. It soon became evident that the pilot needed to be further restricted. Most of the students could perhaps solve problems or find answers, but their understanding of what the answer signified was limited. Many students could not articulate what they did or did not understand about a particular lesson. It became evident that the ability to communicate effectively about mathematics was lacking. I decided to focus on the improvement of the communication skills of students.

With this goal in mind, the students and I began to investigate strategies that might improve their ability to communicate to each other, to me as their teacher, and to others exactly what they knew and did not know about geometry and how this knowledge relates to the world outside the classroom. The first method that came to mind was the use of a math journal. The second idea was a teacher observation rubric to assess what was being communicated within groups in the classroom, using holistic scoring techniques. In addition, the use of videotapes, audiotapes, and checklists was discussed.

The students kept a folder containing all their papers, so we decided to try to put together portfolios consisting of several elements. The first would be journals, which I hoped to begin in mid-November; for the third six-week period, daily grades would consist of journals, graded holistically. By the fourth six-week period, beginning in January, holistic scoring and group grades would be added, and the journal maintained. By the fifth period beginning in March, audiotaping and videotaping would commence, and peer evaluation of communication skills would be added.

Using the Vermont Assessment Portfolio (1990) model, I designed a rough rubric for evaluating written work in journals. The journal entry would be graded on a four-point scale based on fluency and elaboration. The only instruction given for the first few days of journal entries was simply "Write." The products emerging from the first several days of journal entries were very disheartening. The students evidently had little idea or cared very little about what should go into their entries. I then modified the instruction to give more structure to what was written and used sentence completion items such as:

- I see how this lesson can help me later in life if I . . .
- I think triangles (or whatever) are interesting because . . .
- I really wish I knew more about . . .
- If I only knew . . .
- The color of geometry is . . .

The students were then required to write a paragraph elaborating on this statement. The time allowed was about ten minutes daily. The results from this period, which lasted about two weeks, were somewhat better. The samples were becoming coherent, more concise, and more elaborate. I observed that students were able to explain to their peers and to me exactly what they did or did not know. This level was considered satisfactory and was maintained throughout the year.

The next step in improving communication involved the use of mathematical language, symbols, properties, and postulates. A holistic grading system, again adapted from the Vermont project, was developed for proofs and problems. My students balked at the idea of a two-column proof (as do most geometry students). We started out in small steps, writing down "What I know and why I know it." When stating these facts verbally and in writing for the class, the students were unknowingly doing paragraph proofs. They were graded by their peers on a one-to-four-point scale for clarity, sequence, and elaboration. Finally, the two-column proof was developed. Students had previously placed theorems on note cards. The note cards were then used to make a flow chart sequencing the proof. Students were encouraged to try alternate routes to prove statements. The proofs were graded holistically.

The students were videotaped discussing problems and working in groups; however, this method did not lend itself too readily to this class.

Students were self-conscious and did not talk readily. More frequent use of the video camera might have forestalled this anxiety, but the case became moot when the school's video camera was stolen in February. Audiotapes were not used.

The implementation of a student portfolio was more difficult than I had imagined. I wanted the following items to be in a portfolio: sample early work, sample work from December, sample work from March, a proof, a construction problem, a research problem, an extended-thinking problem, and two more items selected by the student. By contrast, the students wanted to include only those items on which they made the best grades. I therefore compromised: if the student did not want to include a particular item in the portfolio, then it didn't go in. I had established the practice of conferring with the students privately on a weekly basis so we could decide together what would go in the portfolio as well as discuss their progress in general. As the year progressed, time got away from me, and I discontinued these conferences and abandoned the portfolios.

The reaction of the students to the use of different methods of assessment was predictable. The bottom line was "How does this affect my grade?" Many students were uncomfortable with a score that was not immediately translated into a percentage. Nearly every student complained loudly that the journal was unnecessary and that "this is a math class, not English." As time progressed, they became more at ease with the process and valued it. Parents were supportive when it was made clear to them that these methods offered extended and varied opportunities for students to succeed.

This limited pilot of alternative assessment techniques was a success. My students and I have had many opportunities to demonstrate that learning is taking place. The key element is prior planning and commitment. I am very pleased with student progress in the area of communication. As this element was a priority, it received the most time and was not abandoned, merely refined. I intend to incorporate some of these activities into all math classes. The portfolio element was more complex and should have been started on a much smaller scale using only one or two assessment criteria.

It is evident that employing alternative assessment methods and associated rubrics benefits the students in a variety of ways. I would recommend that mathematics teachers begin to employ these techniques and slowly incorporate them into their assessment repertoire. Teachers need training in the use of these methods, and they need to see them demonstrated in a classroom setting. I would strongly suggest ongoing staff development in this area. A network of teachers using innovative evaluation techniques would also be beneficial. I see alternative assessments as an opportunity to meet the needs of students as we work together to produce the future.

Assessing Reasonableness of Answers in Algebra I
Cyndy Zoch
La Grange High School

La Grange is a small town of approximately four thousand people who are very supportive of the school and very concerned with its operation. The high school has approximately 475 students.

The class that I chose for this project is an algebra I class, consisting of fifteen students. One of the students is Hispanic; the rest are white. I have six freshmen, eight sophomores, and one junior. The ability levels in this class range from below average to very high. The very weak students had dropped the class either early in the year or at the end of the semester. In general, the freshmen are much stronger academically than the sophomores. Most of the sophomores came from a freshman prealgebra course, which they had struggled to pass.

It is interesting to notice the different factors motivating the freshmen and sophomores. The sophomores are more motivated by outside influences—band, cheerleading, Future Farmers of America, sports, and the like—whereas the freshmen are intrinsically motivated. While they are involved in extracurricular activities, the driving force behind their good grades is their desire to succeed. Therefore, they strive for the A's while the sophomores struggle for the C's.

The algebra I class is taught third period, just before lunch. Each class day is basically formatted the same way. First, the students work on a warm-up, while I check the roll, verify completion of homework, and pass back papers. The warm-up is usually a unique or unusual problem that requires them to think. I like to find problems that use the skills the students have been learning in a new context. For example, when we were solving systems of equations, I presented the following problem:

Bert's Burger Barn has the following items on its menu:
1 hamburger, 1 french fries, 1 Coke $1.88
1 hamburger, 2 fries $1.93
2 hamburgers, 1 Coke $2.37
How much do the hamburger, french fries, and Coke cost separately?

While they are working on the warm-up, I walk around the room checking homework. This is a completion check, where one of three grades is possible: 100, 70, or 0. Checking homework in this way accomplishes several things. First, a student is not afraid to try all the problems, knowing that he or she could still receive a 100, even if not all the answers are correct. Second, it gives me a considerable amount of time since I no longer grade homework papers. And third, I know at the beginning of the class how much trouble the students had with the homework and whether or not I need to do some more teaching on that topic.

Once the students have finished the warm-up, I call out answers to the homework so that students can find out how well they understood the assignment. They are expected to check their answers and make note of any problems they missed. Once I have called out all the answers, they can request problems to be worked on the board, either by me or by student volunteers.

After checking homework, I either give a quiz or lecture on new material. The lecture usually consists of defining new terms, presenting theorems or rules, and showing examples. I then put three or four sample problems on the board for the students to practice before they begin their homework. They work the problems individually in their notebooks, and I will either walk around the room, answering questions and checking solutions, or I will show the situation on the board, making explanations as I go. Once the lecture and practice are complete, I try to allow the students five to ten minutes to start their homework. This is their last chance to ask questions and get the procedure down before working on their own at home.

I generally assign homework every night, except for the night before a test. My purpose in giving homework is to have the students practice the skill that I taught that day. I firmly believe that they will never learn simply by watching me; they must practice on their own. I like to give short quizzes (five to ten problems) that cover one or two recent topics two to three times a week. I use the quizzes to evaluate how well the students are doing with a particular topic and to decide if I need to do further teaching before I move on to the next section. The quizzes give the students feedback on their understanding of the material as well as an idea of what types of questions to expect on the chapter test. I give tests at the end of every chapter, which usually means two tests per six weeks. The tests primarily provide my grade for each student. They count 40 percent of the six-week grade, whereas quizzes count 20 percent and homework 10 percent. I place so much emphasis on tests because I feel the student must understand all of the pieces in a chapter and the ways they relate to be successful in that area. The only other type of test I give is the six-week exam required by the school district. This test counts as 25 percent of their grade and usually covers everything that has been taught thus far in the current semester.

Assessment Plan

In my initial assessment plan, which I began implementing at the start of the second semester, my goal was to enable students to evaluate the reasonableness of an answer. I intended to change how I evaluated warm-ups, tests, and the checking of homework. In the area of warm-ups, I intended to have the students keep a journal in which they would record the thought processes used in solving the problem as well as an explanation of why they believed their answer was correct. I planned to use a scale-rating system (from one to five) to grade the warm-ups and also to provide feedback; the students could then see how they might have worked the problem differently or better or how they could have solved it using skills they learned in algebra class.

On tests, I intended to add a question to every word problem: "Do you think your answer is reasonable? Explain why or why not." In answering this question, the student could receive points for answering the problem incorrectly if he or she could tell me why the solution was wrong.

My initial plan also called for a change in the way I checked homework. I planned to have the students check over their answers with a partner, find one problem for which they had different solutions, and then rework the problem until they could determine which answer is correct. The work involved would be recorded in their journals. I hoped that by going through this process, the students would learn how to find their own mistakes and how to prevent them from occurring again.

The first step I made toward the implementation of my plan was to purchase little notebooks for each student to use as a journal. Their first assignment in the journal was to reflect on their first semester in algebra I: how they did, what they liked, what they did not like, what they would like to see more or less of, and so forth. I probably did not fully understand any of my students until after I had read these entries. I learned how they felt about themselves and math, what areas they had problems with, and what I did that they liked or did not like. One student wrote, "I like it when you tell me I'm smart. It makes me feel good." Until then, I never realized how much weight my words carry with my students.

From then on, the journals were used primarily to record answers to warm-ups, although occasionally I did have the students write down how well they thought they understood a certain topic and what parts were still giving them trouble. I never did get around to using a rating system for grading the journals. I found that so many of my students still just gave an answer even if I asked for a detailed explanation. Those who did attempt an explanation had a very hard time expressing their thoughts and usually ended up providing too little information. I realized that this process of having students explain their thinking was going to take a lot of effort and time and should really be implemented at the beginning of the school year instead of the middle, when the students had already settled into a routine. I did try, whenever feasible, to explain to the students how a warm-up might have been solved using the algebra skills they were learning, but I never insisted that they use that method to solve the problem.

On a couple of tests that had word problems, I added, "Do you think your answer is correct? Explain." I found that all of the students could tell me correctly if their answer was right or wrong and even how they knew. Those who did get it wrong were still not able to find the right answer; they just knew they had the wrong one. If I removed this question from the word problem, the students made no noticeable attempt on their own to verify whether or not the answer was correct or even if it made sense given the restrictions of the problem. Again, I believe the students need to be trained in this procedure from the very beginning.

I did not attempt my idea of changing how homework was checked. I felt the class would not have put in the effort needed. They tend to visit too much when placed in small groups or pairs. However, an idea not in the original plan that I did implement was boardwork. After I lectured, I found that if I asked the students whether they had any questions, they would say no, they understood. But later that night, they would not be able to work the problems. This semester, I tried to get them to work at the board as much as possible. Working at the board forces the students actually to attempt the problem because they know that I am watching, and it makes them realize they may not fully understand how to work the problem. It allows me to see every student at once, so that I can determine who needs more help.

When I first mentioned this project to my students, they were very open to the idea. They did not mind being videotaped, filling out the surveys, and trying out all of my experiments. They liked some of the ideas better than others, however. They had a very hard time putting down on paper the steps they used in solving a problem. This process was something not previously asked of them; it will take a long time for them to become comfortable with and accomplished at this procedure. At the same time, they did seem to like writing in their journals how they felt about the class or about the topic we were discussing. I plan to use journals next year in all my classes as a tool to open communication between me and my students. I want to hear how they feel and what they think, and journals seem to be the best way, short of individual conferences. The students also liked working at the board. They liked being out of their desks and actively participating. They did not experience peer pressure because no one was sitting at the desks watching them — everyone but me was at the board. I hope to continue this practice next year, although it may not be possible if the class gets much larger. The biggest difficulty I encountered was in getting myself and the students to change our ways in the middle of the year. I found that we were all comfortable with the way in which we had been doing things. If I tried something new and the students were even the slightest bit vocal in their disagreement, I tended to drop it rather than pursue it further.

While I feel that some of the alternatives do not apply to high school students (for example, portfolios), I do believe that the high school math teacher has many effective selections to choose from. My recommendations to other teachers who would like to use alternative assessments are to plan early: decide what instruments to use for evaluation; determine how to grade, if at all; prepare the students; start at the beginning of the year; and be flexible. The first and last steps are the most important. Before implementing any new assessments, a teacher must be sure to plan far in advance what will be done, how it will be done, and how it will be evaluated. My biggest problem was that I never allowed myself enough time for what I wanted to do. Once a teacher has begun using alternative assessments, it is very important to be open to how well they are working. If the teacher or the students are not comfortable with the new technique or if it is not working for whatever reason, throw it out! Do not be afraid to start over. Just be sure that the students are aware of what is being done and why.

14

EFFECTS OF ALTERNATIVE ASSESSMENT IN MATHEMATICS CLASSROOMS

RECENT EXPERIENCE IN AMERICAN MATHEMATICS EDUCATION SEEMS TO VERIFY that the material tested is the material taught. The evidence from the 1987 National Assessment of Educational Progress (NAEP), for example, has shown that computational skills have been the focus of competency tests, spawning textbooks and instructional emphases aimed at developing these skills in students. Teachers have been legitimately concerned that if they "fight the system" and teach higher-order thinking, their students would suffer on the computationally oriented tests they are required to pass. Many educators believe that very little change will occur in mathematics curricula and teaching without a concurrent change in testing, especially in state and national standardized tests used to assess and compare student, school, and district performances (Kulm, 1990).

Mathematics educators have called for new approaches to assessment and provided some directions for change. Promising work on developing new approaches to mathematics evaluation has begun to appear at the national, state, and local levels. However, little research has been done on specific approaches to this assessment and the ways they work with various student populations.

Most mathematics teachers believe that higher-order thinking is important. In the Second International Mathematics Study (IMS), more than 60 percent of U.S. mathematics teachers listed their highest goal as "developing a systematic approach to solving problems and developing an awareness of the importance of mathematics in everyday life" (Crosswhite, Dossey, Swafford, McKnight, & Cooney, 1986). Student performance on the IMS and recent NAEP tests indicate, however, that the aspirations of teachers and the performance of their students are very different things. Apparently, teachers are unable to accomplish what they would like to do.

Why do mathematics teachers not reach their goals for teaching higher-order thinking? There are several possibilities. Teachers may be trying to teach higher-order thinking, but the students cannot learn; teachers may think they are teaching higher-order content but are actually teaching rote application of methods to solve special classes of word problems; state and local tests may demand that teachers do other things; or teachers may not know how to evaluate student progress toward and achievement of higher-order thinking. All of these explanations are probably true to some extent for many teachers. However, confronting the last issue—learning how to evaluate higher-order mathematical thinking—would go a long ways toward overcoming other barriers. Successful teaching of anything, including higher-order thinking in mathematics, is dependent upon the ability to determine the degree to which it has been learned. Valid and usable tests can provide an impetus for teaching higher-order skills.

In this project, the goal was to bring instruction and assessment into closer alignment and interaction. This alignment was made possible by helping teachers develop the ability to gauge the effects of teaching approaches designed to involve students in problem solving and thinking. Teachers were encouraged to broaden their repertoire of teaching strategies and to use alternative assessment as a part of implementing these strategies. Work on developing alternative assessment plans contributed to bringing teaching and testing into agreement. Instead of being limited by traditional tests, teachers developed plans for assessment that fit within their own styles and approaches.

Teacher Change Model

I was assisted in this portion of the study by two of my graduate students, Bonita McMullen and James Telese. A key objective of this project was to conduct research on the effects of alternative assessment on the activities within teachers' classrooms. (A full report of the project appears in Kulm, Telese, & McMullen [1993].) We wanted to determine whether the use of alternative assessment had an effect on classroom instruction and on students' attitudes toward mathematics. Fennema and Franke (1992) propose a model hypothesizing that teachers' knowledge develops in the classroom context through the dynamic and interactive impact of knowledge of mathematics, of pedagogy, and of learners' cognitions in mathematics. We believe that alternative assessments enhance teachers' understanding in all three of these areas, but especially their knowledge of learners' cognitions and of effective teaching.

In order to observe the outcomes when teachers are empowered by a richer knowledge base, we looked at the three characteristics of mathematics teaching that Peterson (1988) identified as being essential for promoting higher-order thinking. The interplay between the teachers' knowledge, the new knowledge about alternative assessment, and the resulting classroom teaching processes is shown in Figure 14.1.

In this model, knowledge about alternative assessment strategies acts to enrich teachers' knowledge of learners' cognitions. Teachers learn about

Figure 14.1. Teachers' Knowledge: Impact of Alternative Assessment.

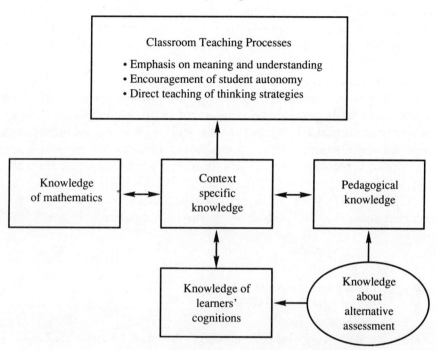

their students' mathematical knowledge, understanding, and problem-solving processes. They also see how students work on extended and complex problems and how they communicate their work through oral, written, graphic, and other approaches. Finally, they learn how students do mathematics in individual and group situations. This enriched and in-depth understanding about students has an impact on teachers' pedagogy. Teaching strategies that were dormant or not well developed become activated and intensified. More traditional teacher-centered approaches are used less often in light of evaluations of their effectiveness in meeting students' cognitive needs. In some instances, knowledge of alternative assessment may also act upon and extend teachers' mathematical knowledge through work in developing tasks and measuring students' mathematical performances.

Data on Teaching

Again, we wanted to see if and how alternative assessment changed what teachers did in the classroom. We also wanted to determine if the new assessment approaches changed students' attitudes about math. In order to find out about the classroom activities the teachers used, we did two things. We collected observation data from all of the classes, and we asked the students in each class what activities they did and how they felt about math. An initial set of observations was done early in the project, prior to teachers' implementation of their assessment strategies. This first observation served to establish baseline data on teaching strategies. During the school year, each of the teachers was observed two more times, once near the middle of the project and once at the end of the school year. These observations provided data that reflected changes in teaching approaches during the year.

The classroom observation instrument that we developed focused on the three processes essential for promoting the learning of higher-order thinking. Special attention was given to characterizing teaching approaches that reflect nontraditional strategies such as problem-based instruction, small-group and other student-centered work, and attention to student learning as opposed to "covering" mathematics content. The observation form is shown in Table 14.1.

The observer rated each item independently using a six-level, process-based scale that addressed the items in approximately the following terminology:

0 — Not present
1 — Implied but not overtly present
2 — Present but not developed
3 — Present and used
4 — Used in an insightful manner but could be expanded
5 — Developed and used; student understanding clear

The more subtle classroom activities such as refining hypotheses or enjoying mathematics were more difficult to rate since they cannot always be recognized within one limited classroom visit. However, over a series of visits, these items began to be more recognizable.

After the lesson, we also asked the teachers to rate themselves on each of the observation items. These ratings were discussed with the teacher as part of the postlesson interview session. This self-rating helped to focus the teachers' attention on the types of teaching strategies identified as enhancing higher-order thinking skills in students. Finally, each observation was videotaped. The videotapes were used in a reliability analysis of the observation ratings. Clips from the videotapes are also useful for demonstrating examples of instructional activities that lead to higher-order thinking.

Each teacher kept a journal of his or her classroom work and activities, focusing on assessment implementation. The journals were handed in at each class meeting. There were no specific guidelines for the journals, but teachers were encouraged to record their approaches to assessment, the ways they worked, reflections on special areas of interest, good ideas, special classroom episodes, or any other information that would reveal the progress of implementing their assessment plans. Many of the journals described the types of assignments and activities used to evaluate student learning and the reactions of both themselves and their students as they made these changes.

Samples of classroom tests used by the teachers were collected at the

Table 14.1. Innovative Mathematics Assessment Project Observation Form.

Teacher: _____ Date: _____

Class: _____ Time: _____

Emphasis on meaning and understanding	*Rating*

Communicates that math problems cannot always be solved quickly.

Communicates that some problems have more than one answer.

Focuses on what students do know rather than what they don't know.

Uses informal assessment to provide feedback to students.

Emphasizes that mathematics is useful and makes sense.

Includes mathematical processes used in context rather than in isolation.

Emphasizes understanding of mathematical concepts.

Provides opportunities to restate and formulate problems.

Provides opportunities to ask questions, consider different possibilities.

Expresses mathematics through pictures, diagrams, graphs, words, symbols, or numerical examples.

Uses a variety of mathematical tools, models, manipulatives, calculators, or computers.

Provides opportunities for students to plan, invent, or design mathematical ideas, projects, activities, or products.

Encouragement of students' autonomy and persistence	*Rating*

Students learn at their own pace.

Students who perform with difficulty are not labeled as failures.

All students are expected to be able to learn mathematics.

Students work on extended assignments or investigations.

Speed is not an important factor in determining students' achievement.

Students are encouraged to think and be persistent and self-directed.

Students work together to develop mathematical thinking skills.

Direct teaching of higher-order cognitive strategies	*Rating*

Teacher helps students to formulate and refine hypotheses.

Opportunities are given for collecting and organizing data and information.

Teacher helps students to learn and practice a variety of strategies for doing mathematics.

Teacher encourages students to reflect on their own problem-solving methods and strategies.

Students are asked to explain concepts orally or in writing.

Opportunities are given to work with open-ended or poorly defined real-life problems.

Students are provided situations in which they enjoy doing mathematics.

end of the project. These items were to provide indicators of how extensively the teachers actually implemented the innovative assessment approaches. Of special interest was whether the new approaches began to permeate the day-to-day classroom quizzes and tests and whether the classroom tests showed variety in their formats and settings.

Results of Effects on Teaching

During the year, our discussions with the teachers made it clear that there were varying plans and implementations according to grade level. Alternative assessment goals and strategies at the elementary school, for example, were different from those used by high school teachers. It therefore made sense to look at the teachers' observation data according to grade level. We decided to group the teacher data into elementary (grades four through six), middle (grades seven and eight), and high school (grades nine and ten). The mean ratings for each grade-level group were calculated separately for the three sets of processes on the observation form. In order to see changes over the year, we looked at the mean rating for each observation.

Graphs of the means for the meaning and understanding processes show what happened (see Figure 14.2). Over the period of the project, the teachers increased their use of activities aimed at meaning and understanding. The sharpest increase occurred between the second and third observations, when the teachers were well along in using alternative assessments in their classes. Teachers at all grade levels showed a similar pattern of improvement. The elementary teachers began the project using more of these processes and continued to improve, ending the year with the highest mean.

Graphs for each observation of the encouragement of student autonomy and persistence process (Figure 14.3) again show that the elementary, middle school, and high school means follow the same pattern of improvement, with significant improvements from observation two to three. The elementary teachers were at the top, improving during the last half of the year. The middle and high school teachers also demonstrated great improvement, with the middle-grade teachers ranking second and high school teachers ranking third by the end of the year.

The graphs for direct teaching of higher-order cognitive strategies (Figure 14.4) indicate similar patterns of improvement for each grade level. At first, the elementary teachers decreased somewhat in this area before taking a sharp upward swing by the end of the year. The middle school paralleled the high school over the year and ended with the second highest level of direct teaching of thinking strategies.

Data from Students

Student questionnaires provided another measure of whether teachers changed their teaching and assessment approaches. On the same schedule

Figure 14.2. Graph of Cell Means for
Meaning and Understanding Teaching Processes at Three Observations.

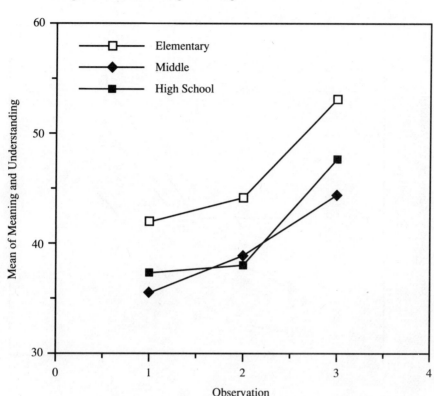

as the observations (at the beginning, middle, and end of the year), students were given a 25-item questionnaire. The first ten items were aimed at determining whether the innovative testing approaches had an impact on the way students viewed mathematics. The last fifteen questions provided information, from the students' point of view, on whether teachers' classroom practices changed as a result of the assessment work. The questions asked are shown in Table 14.2.

The last fifteen questions were categorized according to whether they reflected traditional (TACT scale) or nontraditional (NACT scale) teaching activities. The TACT scale includes items 11, 12, 15, 16, 18, 19, 21, and 25. The NACT scale consists of items 13, 14, 15, 17, 18, 20, 21, 22, 23, 24, and 25. Note that items 15, 18, 21, and 25 are included on both scales, since they can be interpreted as describing types of activity relevant to each scale. Separate scores were computed for each. Table 14.3 shows the means of the attitude and teaching activity scales for each observation.

The overall attitude means showed improvement from survey one to survey three. When teachers implemented alternative assessment items aligned with instructional practices, positive attitudes toward mathematics

Figure 14.3. Graph of Cell Means for Encouragement of
Student Autonomy and Persistence Teaching Processes at Three Observations.

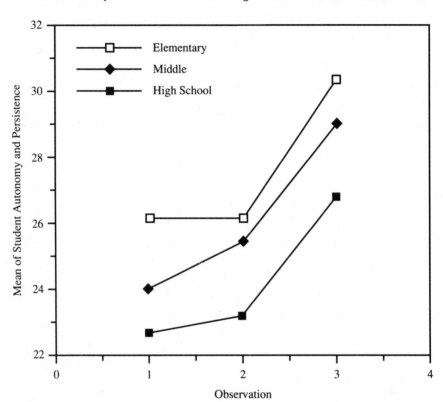

developed. The students' responses showed that teachers used more non-traditional teaching activities than traditional ones, a factor contributing to the overall improvement in their attitudes.

More detailed analysis was done that compared the responses of boys and girls and of grade levels and ethnic groups. Both the female and male students indicated an increase in the nontraditional teaching activities, but the females saw a greater change than the males. This result suggests that female students may not view what goes on in mathematics class in the same way as males. Traditionally, female students tend to feel ignored, receive less encouragement, and have lower achievement in mathematics. However, in this study, where nontraditional teaching methods in the classroom were used, female students perceived greater involvement in these activities. In many studies of gender differences in mathematics, female students also have poorer attitudes toward mathematics than male students. In this study, female students' attitudes toward mathematics improved, remaining at the same level as males'. Alternative assessment techniques, aligned with instruction, appear to contribute to female students' greater involvement in and improved attitudes toward mathematics.

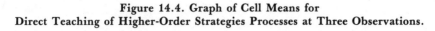

Figure 14.4. Graph of Cell Means for
Direct Teaching of Higher-Order Strategies Processes at Three Observations.

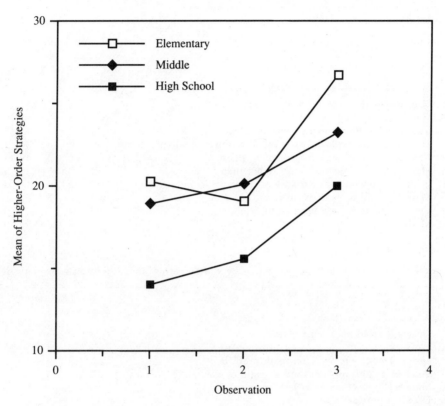

Results at the various grade levels were interesting, particularly at the high school level. The high school group showed a large increase in attitude score from observation one to three. This was surprising since, according to their teachers, the high school group appeared to resist the change to nontraditional teaching practices. Yet these students showed the greatest improvement in attitude score. Those at the elementary level showed a slight improvement in attitudes and in nontraditional teaching activities. This finding may result from the fact that elementary school students normally experience hands-on activities, group work, and other nontraditional mathematics as part of their normal class activities. The seventh- and eighth-grade classes showed a slight improvement in attitude and nontraditional teaching activities from survey one to survey two.

Each of the ethnic groups had positive changes in attitudes and saw more nontraditional activities from survey one to survey three. African-American students maintained a slightly higher attitude score than Asian students, white students, and Hispanic students. Nevertheless, alternative assessment techniques improved student attitudes toward mathematics regardless of ethnic background. Again, this outcome implies that when

Table 14.2. Student Survey.

Attitudes About Math

Mark the choice that best describes your feeling or opinion about each statement.

		Rating			
	Disagree				*Agree*
1. Learning math is mostly memorizing.	1	2	3	4	5
2. Math is interesting.	1	2	3	4	5
3. Guessing is OK in solving math problems.	1	2	3	4	5
4. There is always a rule or two to follow in solving math problems.	1	2	3	4	5
5. New discoveries are seldom made in math.	1	2	3	4	5
6. Math is mostly about symbols rather than ideas.	1	2	3	4	5
7. In math, knowing why an answer is correct is important.	1	2	3	4	5
8. Math is useful in everyday life.	1	2	3	4	5
9. I would like to have a job that uses math.	1	2	3	4	5
10. Math is fun.	1	2	3	4	5

Activities in Math Class

Mark the choice that best describes how often you do each of these things in your math class.

		How Often			
	Never				*A Lot*
11. Do math problems from the textbook.	1	2	3	4	5
12. Work alone at my desk on math problems.	1	2	3	4	5
13. Use a computer to work on math problems.	1	2	3	4	5
14. Work on math problems with a group of classmates.	1	2	3	4	5
15. Show all of my work on a test or quiz.	1	2	3	4	5
16. Do math practice worksheets.	1	2	3	4	5
17. Play math games.	1	2	3	4	5
18. Have class discussions about math problems.	1	2	3	4	5
19. Watch the teacher work problems on the board.	1	2	3	4	5
20. Do math projects.	1	2	3	4	5
21. Take math tests and quizzes.	1	2	3	4	5
22. Talk to the teacher about how I am doing in math.	1	2	3	4	5
23. Make up my own math problems to solve.	1	2	3	4	5
24. Use calculators to solve math problems.	1	2	3	4	5
25. Explain how you solve math problems.	1	2	3	4	5

teachers use nontraditional teaching activities, student attitudes toward mathematics improve.

In summary, the results from the student surveys indicate that when teachers are exposed to alternative assessment techniques, they will adjust their teaching activities to coincide with these techniques, and positive consequences result. Students, whether male or female, and regardless of ethnic background, develop desirable attitudes toward mathematics instruction. Also, female students tend to become more involved in mathematics discourse when experiencing nontraditional teaching activities, as did other students. High school students view the teaching changes as being significantly greater than the lower grade levels.

Table 14.3. Means from Student Survey Instrument.

	Observation 1		Observation 2		Observation 3	
	N	Mean	N	Mean	N	Mean
Attitude	379	33.09	368	33.73	196	34.31
TACT	374	30.39	363	30.63	190	29.97
NACT	371	34.44	363	36.13	187	36.51

Summary of Outcomes

In this project, we made significant progress in developing teachers' knowledge of how to evaluate problem solving and other types of higher-order thinking. This knowledge appears to provide teachers with the freedom to choose and implement instructional activities that enhance higher-order thinking. These teachers began to find ways in which they could achieve their own and their schools' goals of teaching for conceptual understanding, problem solving, and reasoning in mathematics.

We found that when teachers used alternative approaches to asessment, they also changed their teaching. Teachers increased their use of strategies that research has found to promote students' higher-order thinking. They did activities that enhanced meaning and understanding, developed student autonomy and independence, and helped students learn problem-solving strategies. Students' attitudes toward math improved. Students reported being more involved in doing group work, using calculators, making up their own problems, and engaging in other activities that reflect active rather than passive mathematics learning.

Teachers provided feedback at the end of the project, outlining some of the abilities, knowledge, and skills they had developed. They reported learning a variety of approaches for helping students learn basic mathematical facts and skills. The teachers said they were more able to

- Foresee students' problems in computational skills and emphasize steps to overcome these problem areas
- Develop a system of homework and quizzes to give an accurate description of students' abilities
- Give different forms of assessment, involving students in showing and explaining their work
- Ask probing questions to encourage students to arrive at the correct answer
- Use questioning techniques that uncover students' errors
- Use multiple approaches in assessing students' knowledge and skills
- Develop and use rubrics to score student work
- Feel comfortable in allowing students to use models and manipulatives

Teachers also developed knowledge of strategies for teaching mathematical reasoning and problem solving. They reported feeling more capable in

- Selecting open-ended problems that met the students' levels of experience and that systematically built problem difficulty
- Using open-ended problems to evaluate problem-solving ability
- Looking for alternative methods and approaches
- Spending time discussing problem-solving strategies
- Helping children overcome their fear of thinking
- Requiring students to engage daily in problem solving and requiring them to demonstrate and communicate understandings in mathematics — orally and in writing
- Focusing on process rather than simply on answers
- Being willing to try new ideas
- Using questioning techniques and encouraging the students to expand on answers and ideas
- Being able to follow the thought processes of all students
- Working with students one on one

Although most of the teachers indicated that they still had much to learn about alternative approaches to assessment, they felt confident in trying further ideas and expressed the desire to implement these in the coming year. Many of the teachers believed they could be even more successful if they were to put these strategies into practice at the beginning of the school year.

Information about new approaches to mathematics assessment at the classroom level is critical for further progress in reforming mathematics education. If student performance on national, state, and local assessments is to meet the expectations of new standards, instruction and assessment must be closely linked. This study provided evidence that in-service work on alternative assessment can pay dividends in helping mathematics teachers use approaches that enhance higher-order thinking processes.

References

Arter, J. (1993, April). *Designing scoring rubrics for performance assessments: The heart of the matter.* Paper presented at the annual meeting of the American Educational Research Association, Atlanta, GA.

Assessment of Performance Unit. (1980.) Mathematical development (Secondary Survey Report, No. 1). London, England: HMSO.

Baker, E. L. (1990). Developing comprehensive assessments of higher order thinking. In G. Kulm (Ed.), *Assessing higher order thinking in mathematics* (pp. 7–20). Washington, DC: American Association for the Advancement of Science Press.

Baron, J. B. (1992). Performance-based assessment in mathematics and science. (Connecticut Common Core of Learning Mathematics Assessment Program). New Haven: Connecticut State Department of Education.

Bell, A. W., Costello, J., & Kuchemann, P. (1983). *Review of research in mathematical education* (Pt. A). Berkshire, England: Nfer-Nelson.

Carpenter, T. P. (1986). Conceptual knowledge as a foundation for procedural knowledge. In J. Heibert (Ed.), *Conceptual and procedural knowledge: The case of mathematics* (pp. 113–132). Hillsdale, NJ: Erlbaum.

Collison, J. (1992). Using performance assessment to determine mathematical dispositions. *Arithmetic Teacher, 39,* 40–47.

Crosswhite, F. J., Dossey, J. A., Swafford, J. O., McKnight, C. C., & Cooney, T. J. (1986). (Second International Mathematics Study Summary Report for the United States). Champaign: University of Illinois.

DeStefano, L. (1993). Cross-scorer and cross-method comparability and distribution of judgments of student math, reading, and writing performance: Results from the New Standards Project Big Sky Scoring Conference. (Technical Report). Champaign: University of Illinois.

Ernest, P. (1992). *Mathematics teaching: State of the art.* New York: Elsevier Press.

Fennema, E., & Franke, M. L. (1992). Teachers' knowledge and its impact. In D. Grouws (Ed.), *Handbook of research on mathematics teaching and learning* (pp. 147–164). New York: Macmillan.

Flavell, J. H. (1976). Metacognitive aspects of problem solving. In L. Resnick (Ed.), *The nature of intelligence.* Hillsdale, NJ: Erlbaum.

Friel, S. J., Mokros, J. R., & Russell, J. (1992). *Used numbers: Real data in the classroom.* Palo Alto, CA: Seymour.

Gardner, H. (1992). Assessment in context: The alternative to standardized testing. In B. Gifford & M. O'Connor (Eds.), *Changing assessments: Alternative views of aptitude, achievement, and instruction.* Boston: Kluwer.

Johnson, D. W., & Johnson, R. T. (1991). Group assessment as an aid to science instruction. In G. Kulm & S. M. Malcom (Eds.), *Science assessment in the service of reform* (pp. 283–289). Washington, DC: American Association for the Advancement of Science Press.

Kulm, G. (Ed.). (1990). *Assessing higher order thinking in mathematics.* Washington, DC: American Association for the Advancement of Science Press.

Kulm, G., & Lockmandy, T. (1976). An alternative approach to evaluating math achievement. *Indiana Mathematics Newsletter 39,* 1–4.

Kulm, G., & Malcom, S. M. (Eds.). (1991). *Science assessment in the service of reform.* Washington, DC: American Association for the Advancement of Science Press.

Kulm, G., Telese, J., & McMullen, B. (1993). Innovative mathematics assessment project. (Final Report). College Station: Texas A&M University.

Maryland State Department of Education, Division of Instruction. (1992). Maryland School Performance Assessment Program. Annapolis: Author.

McKnight, C. C., Crosswhite, F. J., Dossey, J. A., Kifer, E., Swafford, J. A., Travers, K. J., & Cooney, T. J. (1987). *The underachieving curriculum.* Champaign, IL: Stipes.

Miller, R. (1992). *Testing for learning.* New York: Free Press.

National Assessment of Educational Progress. (1987). *Learning by doing: A manual for teaching and assessing higher-order thinking in science and mathematics.* Princeton, NJ: Author.

National Council of Teachers of Mathematics. (1989). *Curriculum and evaluation standards for school mathematics.* Reston, VA: Author.

National Council of Teachers of Mathematics. (1991). *Professional standards for teaching mathematics.* Reston, VA: Author.

National Council of Teachers of Mathematics. (1993). *Assessment standards for school mathematics: Working draft.* Reston, VA: Author.

Pandey, T. (1990). Power items and the alignment of curriculum and assessment. In G. Kulm (Ed.), *Assessing higher order thinking in mathematics* (pp. 39–51). Washington, DC: American Association for the Advancement of Science Press.

Pandey, T. (1991). *A sampler of mathematics assessment.* Sacramento: California State Department of Education.

Peterson, P. L. (1988). Teaching for higher-order thinking. In T. J. Cooney & D. Jones (Eds.), *Effective mathematics teaching.* Reston, VA: National Council of Teachers of Mathematics.

Polya, G. (1957). *How to solve it.* New York: Doubleday.

Reimer, L., & Reimer, W. (1990). *Mathematicians are people too: Stories from the lives of great mathematicians.* Palo Alto, CA: Seymour.

Schoenfeld, A. (1983). Beyond the purely cognitive: Belief systems, social cognitions, and metacognitions as driving forces in intellectual performance. *Cognitive Science, 7,* 329–363.

Stenmark, J. K. (1989). *Assessment alternatives in mathematics.* Berkeley: University of California.

Stenmark, J. K. (1992). *Mathematics assessment: Myths, models, good questions, and practical suggestions.* Reston, VA: National Council of Teachers of Mathematics.

Tsuruda, G. (1992). Problem of the week: Writing to develop mathematical power. Presentation at the National Council of Teachers of Mathematics 70th annual meeting, Nashville, TN.

Useem, E. L. (1991). Tracking students out of advanced mathematics. *The Education Digest, 56,* 54–58.

Vermont State Board of Education. (1990). *Looking beyond the answer: Report of Vermont's mathematics portfolio assessment program.* Montpelier: Author.

Index